# CONAN DOYLE BIBLIOGRAPHY

A Bibliography of the Works of
Sir Arthur Conan Doyle
M.D., LL.D. (1859-1930)

By
Gaby Goldscheider

*Privately published by*
Gaby Goldscheider . 29 Temple Road . Windsor
1977

ISBN 0 9505725 0 0

Printed by Stoate & Bishop (Printers) Ltd., Gloucester & Cheltenham

## FOREWORD

About a year ago, when I became interested in Conan Doyle and his books, I found, to my amazement, that no-one had attempted a bibliography since Locke had published his in 1928.[1] Locke's Bibliographical Catalogue, however, is by no means complete. By that I do not mean that it stops at 1928, but that there are quite a number of gaps. Pierre Nordon in his biography of Conan Doyle[2] gives the reader a supplementary list, which I have incorporated into mine.

Locke's Bibliography is not easily available, and has long been out of print. In 1974, The New York Graphic Society published a vast tome entitled: *The World Bibliography of Sherlock Holmes and Dr. Watson*,[3] which can be consulted in connexion with anything pertaining to Sherlock Holmes: books, magazines, plays, films, radio programmes, societies, and all kinds of memorabilia. The fact that it lists over 6,000 items in 50 languages shows that Holmesiana has indeed become a worldwide cult. But that Conan Doyle's other works have been omitted, even in their first editions, indicates that it was high time for someone to write a new bibliography of the works of this most remarkable of men. Doyle made a great contribution to literature, not only by his vast output, but because he *was* a highly gifted and serious writer. His interests were as varied as Leonardo's and his vision as clear at times as Blake's — though these comparisons are not to be taken too seriously !— but certainly, his writings show moments of pure genius. One cannot divorce the creator from his creations. Conan Doyle and Sherlock Holmes are one and the same being, which cannot and must not be torn apart.

Time and opportunity have not allowed me to write the comprehensive bibliography I originally intended. All I have attempted to do here is to collect as much information as I could readily obtain, but which, I hope, will nevertheless prove to be a useful checklist for librarians, collectors, booksellers, scholars and students alike. Any help with further information and corrections for a revised edition will be gratefully received.

I have concentrated mainly on including as many works of The Master as I could track down in the true Holmesian tradition: — they total some 500. Quite an impressive number for one man to have written in his lifetime. I have not concerned myself overmuch with Holmesiana, as this is so excellently covered by *The World Bibliography*. But for those readers whose interest lies mainly with Sherlock Holmes, I have indicated with an asterisk those titles which concern this illustrious character.

Ronald Pearsall, in his recently published biography of Conan Doyle,[4] states at the end of his bibliography that [after all] . . . 'most important are Doyle's published works which cover an immense range . . .' With this opinion I whole-heartedly agree, but, he adds: 'Most of Doyle's non-Sherlock Holmes books are out of print.' Over this I lament and sincerely hope that publishers will soon realize the need to reprint many of Doyle's fascinating and entertaining stories, thrillers, science fiction, prophetic articles, books of poetry and spiritualist writings. For Conan Doyle is back — there is no doubt of that!

Gaby Goldscheider
Windsor, June 1977

[1]see item 1077
[2]see item 1079
[3]see item 1084
[4]see item 1080

CAPTAIN SHARKEY

# THE WORKS OF THE MASTER

RODNEY STONE

Major works in large print
All publishers, unless otherwise stated, are London-based

***The Abbey Grange [The Adventure of]**
1. **1904.** Story in: The Strand Magazine, Sep. issue; illus. by Sidney Paget
2. **1905.** Story in: The Return of Sherlock Holmes [q.v.]

**About Cricket**
3. **1918.** Story in: The Strand Magazine
4. **1918.** In: Danger! And Other Stories [q.v.]
5. **1923.** In: Three of Them [q.v.]

**The Absolute Proof**
6. **1920.** In: The Strand Magazine

**Actor's Duel and the Winning Shot**
7. **1894.** Published by John Dicks [not in Locke]

ADVENTURE AND MEDICAL LIFE [**Tales of**]
8. **[1922].** Murray; 'Uniform Edition'; first ed; blue paper boards blocked pic. in blind, gilt; 309 pp; 8vo (contains some stories published for the first time)
9. **1928.** Pitman; in Pitman's shorthand; New Era Edition; 94pp; 8vo
10. **1929.** In: The Conan Doyle Stories Omnibus [q.v.]

THE ADVENTURES OF [ETIENNE] GERARD
11. **1902.** In: The Strand Magazine; illus. by W. B. Wollen (serialised)
12. **[1903].** Newnes; first ed., 16 illus. by W. B. Wollen; blue cloth dec. and titled gilt; 374 pp. Cr. 8vo
13. **1903.** McClure, Phillips; first U.S. ed; 16 illus. by W. B. Wollen (in some cases differing from those which appeared in the English ed. — *see* Locke); dark-green cloth, pic. blocked, titled green and gilt; 297 pp; 12 pp. adverts at end, dated 1903; Cr. 8vo
14. **1903.** A. L. Burt Co; N.Y., U.S. Copyright Edition; publ. Sept. 1903; dark-green cloth, pic. blocked in white, lime-green and black and titled lime-green; 297 pp; 8 pp. blank at end; Cr. 8vo
15. **[1911]** Newnes' Sixpenny Copyright Novels No. 208; pic. d.w; Sm. 8vo
16. **1922.** Murray (reprint of first ed.)
17. **1932.** In: The Conan Doyle Historical Romances Omnibus [q.v.]
18. **1949.** Gryphon Books; red cloth, lettered black on spine; 316 pp. Cr. 8vo
19. **1956.** In: The Complete Napoleonic Stories Omnibus [q.v.]

*THE ADVENTURES OF SHERLOCK HOLMES
20. **1891-2.** In: The Strand Magazine, Jul. 1891-Jun. 1892 issues; illus. by Sidney Paget
21. **1892.** Newnes; first ed; 25 illus. by Sidney Paget; light-blue cloth over bevelled boards, pic. blocked with 'Strand Library' motif and titled in black and gilt; 317 pp; 4to
22. **1892.** Newnes; first ed, variant issue: light-blue cloth over bevelled boards, pic. blocked with 'Strand Library' motif, with street name missing in its panel; 4to [scarce — not in Locke]
23. **[1892].** Harper & Bros; N.Y; first U.S. ed; light-blue cross-grained cloth, pic. blocked with a large ornament in dark-blue, titled gilt; Cr. 8vo
24. **1893.** Newnes; Second Edition (similar to first ed.)
25. [*c.* **1893].** Tauchnitz Copyright Edition, Leipzig; 2 vols; Sm. 8vo [not in Locke]
26. **1894.** Newnes; Third Edition (similar to first and second eds.)
27. **1894.** Longmans, Green; Colonial Library Edition; 4th ed; grey cloth, ruled, dec. and titled in brown; Cr. 8vo
28. **1895.** Newnes; 34th, 35th and 40th thou; 25 illus. by Sidney Paget & frontis. by P. Naumann; blue cloth blocked and titled with the 'Strand Library' motif on front cover in black and gilt; gilt lettering on spine; floral e.p.s; 343 pp; 16 pp. publisher's cat. at end (dated 12.96 in ed. of 40th thou.)
29. **1902.** Newnes; Souvenir Edition; pic. dec. cloth, gilt; t.e.g; Cr. 8vo

30. **1908.** Smith, Elder; New Edition; 8 illus. by F. H. Townsend; red cloth, gilt; 285 pp; 10 pp. adverts at end; Cr. 8vo
31. **1914.** Smith, Elder; New Edition; 25 illus. by Sidney Paget; red cloth, gilt; 293 pp; 2 pp. adverts at end; 8vo
32. **1924.** Murray; first Thin Paper Edition; red fine-grain cloth; author's initials on front cover, gilt; spine dec. & titled gilt; 248 pp; Sm. 8vo
33. **1950.** Limited Editions Club; ed. by Edgar W. Smith; cloth-backed boards; 3 vols; slip-case
34. **[n.d.].** Newnes; reprint; publisher's three-quarter green cloth; scarlet sheepskin spine, gilt; t.e.g; Cr. 8vo
35. **[n.d.].** Nelson; frontis. by Noel Pocock; red net-grain cloth, ruled and dec. with publisher's device in blind; 8vo

**Advice to a Young Poet**
36. **1911.** Poem in: Songs of the Road [q.v.]

**All About Naughtiness and Frogs and Historical Pictures**
37. **1918.** In: The Strand Magazine
38. **1923.** In: Three of Them [q.v.]

**Alleged Posthumous Writings of Great Authors**
39. **1927.** In: The Fortnightly Review

**An Alpine Pass on "Ski"**
40. **1894.** In: The Strand Magazine, Jul.-Dec. issues; illus. from photographs
41. **1894.** In: Young Man, Jan. issue
42. **1895.** In: McClure's Magazine, Mar. issue

**The American's Tale**
43. **1879.** In: London Society, Extra Christmas Number; pic. wrappers; Cr .8vo

**Angels of Darkness — A Three-Act Play**
44. **1889-1890.** A reconstruction of the Utah scenes in *A Study in Scarlet*; Unpublished [The House of El Dieff, N.Y. priced the Autograph MS of this play in their recent catalogue "Sherlock Holmes and Sherlockiana, 76 Items" at $50,000.00]

**Anglo-American Reunion**
45. **1900.** A short essay [not in Locke]

**The Arab Steed — A Poem**
46. **1899.** In: Daily News Weekly, No. 1; Saturday, Jul. 1st issue; illus. by Arthur Rackham and another artist; Large folio, folded (also included is a verse from Doyle's Soldier's Prayer [q.v.])
47. **1911.** In: Songs of the Road [q.v.]

**The Athabasca Trail**
48. **1919.** Poem in: The Guards Came Through [q.v.]

**A Ballad of the Ranks**
49. **1898.** Poem in: Songs of Action [q.v.]

**The Banners of Progress**
50. **1911.** Poem in: Songs of the Road [q.v.]

**The Bay Horses**
51. **1911.** Poem in: Songs of the Road [q.v.]

**The Beetle Hunter [The Story of]**
52. **1898.** Story in: The Strand Magazine
53. **1908.** In: Round The Fire Stories [q.v.]

**Behind the Times**
54. **1894.** Story in: Round the Red Lamp [q.v.]

**Bendy's Sermon**
55. **1909.** Poem in: The Strand Magazine; illus. from Facsimiles, Old Prints and Drawings by A. J. Gough
56. **1909.** Poem in: Songs of the Road [q.v.]

***The Beryl Coronet [The Adventure of]**
57. **1892.** Story in: The Strand Magazine, May issue; illus. by Sidney Paget
58. **1892.** Story in: The Adventures of Sherlock Holmes [q.v.]

**Beyond The City**
59. **1892.** Newnes; first ed. [not in Locke]
60. **1892.** Publ. in N.Y; pirated (see p. 99 of *Memories and Adventures* [q.v.])

61. [*c.* **1900**]. Newnes' Copyright Novels (1/6); brown boards, dec. in black front cover & spine; spine titled black; 192 pp; pic. d.w. Sm. 8vo [scarce]
62. **[1912].** Everett's Sevenpenny Library; frontis. & dec. title page; green cloth; spine titled gilt; 192 pp; Sm. 8vo
63. **[1913].** Newnes' Sixpenny Copyright Novels; 124 pp.
*see also* **The Great Shadow and Beyond The City** [q.v.]

**The Bigot**
64. **1919.** Poem in: The Guards Came Through [q.v.]

**Billy Bones**
65. **1923.** In: Three of Them [q.v.]

**Bimbashi Joyce**
*see* **The Debut of Bimbashi Joyce** [q.v.]

**The Black Doctor [The Adventure of]**
66. **1898.** Story in: The Strand Magazine, illus. by J. Finnemore

**The Black Doctor and Other Tales of Terror and Mystery**
67. **1919.** Newnes; first ed. [not in Locke]
68. **1937.** Garden City Pub. Co; N.Y; off-white buckram; red label; dec. spine; gilt lettering; 279 pp. 8vo

***Black Peter [The Adventure of]**
69. **1904.** Story in: The Strand Magazine, Mar. issue; illus. by Sidney Paget
70. **1905.** Story in: The Return of Sherlock Holmes [q.v.]

***The Blanched Soldier [The Adventure of]**
71. **1926.** Story in: The Strand Magazine, Nov. issue; illus. by Howard K. Elcock
72. **1927.** Story in: The Case-Book of Sherlock Holmes [q.v.]

**The Blighting of Sharkey**
73. **1911.** Story in: The Last Galley [q.v.]

**The Blind Archer**
74. **1898.** Poem in: Songs of Action [q.v.]

***The Blue Carbuncle [The Adventure of]**
75. **1892.** Story in: The Strand Magazine, Jan. issue; illus. by Sidney Paget
76. **1892.** Story in: The Adventures of Sherlock Holmes [q.v.]
77. **[1937].** Story in: Century of Thrillers [q.v. item 1007]

**Bones**
78. **1882.** Story in: London Society

**Borrowed Scenes**
79. **1918.** In: Danger! And Other Stories [q.v.]

***The Boscombe Valley Mystery**
80. **1891.** Story in: The Strand Magazine, Oct. issue; illus. by Sidney Paget
81. **1892.** Story in: The Adventures of Sherlock Holmes [q.v.]

**The Bravoes of Market Drayton**
82. **1889.** In: Chambers's Journal, Aug. issue

**The Brazilian Cat [The Story of]**
83. **1898.** Story in: The Strand Magazine; illus. by Sidney Paget
84. **1908.** In: Round The Fire Stories [q.v.]

**Brigadier Garard at Waterloo**
85. **1903.** Story in: The Strand Magazine; illus. by W. B. Wollen
86. **[1903].** In: The Adventures of Gerard [q.v.]

**Brigadier Gerard:— A Romantic Comedy in Four Acts**
87. **1906.** Published by Rosenfield [Nordon, p. 349, dates it as 1910 (unpublished). Locke also dates it as 1910]

**The Brigadier in England**
88. **1903.** In: The Strand Magazine; illus. by W. B. Wollen
89. **[1903].** In: The Adventures of Gerard [q.v.]

**The British Campaigns in Europe 1914-1918**
90. **1928.** Bles; first ed; 2pp. preface by Conan Doyle dated 1928; 44 maps and plans, inc. 10 folding maps; blue cloth, gilt lettering on spine; 1008 pp; 4 pp. adverts at end (inc. many of Conan Doyle's books which were obtainable at the Psychic Bookshop); Demy 8vo

THE BRITISH CAMPAIGN IN FRANCE [AND FLANDERS] 1914-1918
91. **1916.** In: The Strand Magazine (serialised)
92. **1916-1919.** Hodder & Stoughton; first ed; maps and plans; blue cloth, gilt lettered on spine; 6 vols. (vols. 2 & 3 of lighter coloured cloth); Demy 8vo
*see also* **History of the Great War** [q.v.]

**The British Campaign in Italy**
93. **1927.** In: The Fortnightly Review

**Brothers — A Play**
*see* **Halves** [q.v.]

**The Brown Hand [The Story of]**
94. **1899.** Story in: The Strand Magazine; illus. by Sidney Paget
95. **1908.** In: Round The Fire Stories [q.v.]

***The Bruce-Partington Plans [The Adventure of]**
96. **1908.** Story in: The Strand Magazine, Dec. issue; illus. by Arthur Twidle.
97. **1917.** Story in: His Last Bow [q.v.]

**The Bugles of Canada**
98. **1922.** In: The Poems of Arthur Conan Doyle [q.v.]

**The Bully of Brocas Court**
99. **1921.** Story in: The Strand Magazine, Nov. issue

**Burger's Secret**
100. **1898.** Story in: The Sunlight Year Book; red cloth, dec. & titled in black, yellow & white; Cr. 8vo [not in Locke]
101. **1900.** Story in: The Green Flag [q.v.] under the title of: *The New Catacomb*

**By the North Sea**
102. **1909.** Poem in: The Press Album; Murray; first ed; illus; white buckram, pic. blocked & titled gilt; Demy 4to (other contributors: Marie Corelli, Alfred Noyes, etc.)
103. **1909.** As above, variant binding: red cloth, pic. blocked; gilt; Demy 4to
104. **1911.** In: Songs of the Road [q.v.]

THE CAPTAIN OF THE POLE-STAR **[and Other Tales]**
105. **1886.** Story in: Dreamland and Ghostland, Vol III [q.v.]
106. **1890.** Longmans, Green, first ed; dark-blue cloth over bevelled boards; gilt lettered; flowered e.p.s; 315 pp; 16 pp. cat. at end; 8vo
107. [*c.* **1893]**. Tauchnitz Copyright Edition, Leipzig; Sm. 8vo
108. [*c.* **1895]**. Optimus Printing Co; N.Y; 'Handy Classics' series of 'Choice Stories by Famous Authors', No. 15; 32 pp; wrappers [very scarce]
109. **1896.** Longmans, Green; Eighth Edition; red cloth, silver titled; vignette title-page and frontis. by Charles Kerr; Cr. 8vo

110. [*c.* **1896**]. Fenno, N.Y; light-blue cloth, front cover & spine dec. & titled white; Cr. 8vo
111. **[n.d.]** Fenno, N.Y; pic. wrappers, containing photograph of the author; printed on flimsy newsprint [pirated?]
112. **[1908]**. Daily Mail Sixpenny Novels; illus. by Reginald Savage; 106 pp.
113. **[1914]**. Hodder & Stoughton Sevenpenny Library; frontis; beige-brown net-grain cloth, blocked with vertical stripes & publisher's pic. device in blind, gilt; 258 pp; Sm. 8vo
114. **[1914]**. As above, variant binding in red
115. [?]. The Amalgamated Press; Cheap Edition; 3 illus. by Reginald Savage

**Captain Sharkey**
116. **1900.** Story in: The Green Flag [q.v.]

***The Cardboard Box [The Adventure of]**
117. **1891.** Story in: The Strand Magazine; Jan. issue; illus. by Sidney Paget
118. **1894.** Story in: The Memoirs of Sherlock Holmes, first U.S. ed. [q.v.]
119. **1917.** Story in: His Last Bow [q.v.]

***A Case of Identity**
120. **1891.** Story in: The Strand Magazine, Sep. issue; illus. by Sidney Paget
121. **1892.** Story in: The Adventures of Sherlock Holmes [q.v.]
122. **1892.** Story in: The Sign of Four. A Scandal in Bohemia — And Other Stories [q.v.]
123. [*c.* **1895**]. Optimus Printing Co; N.Y; 'Handy Classics' series of 'Choice Stories by Famous Authors', No. 10; wrappers; 30 pp.

**The Case of Lady Sannox**
124. **1893.** Story in: The Idler Magazine, Nov. issue
125. **1894.** Story in: Round The Red Lamp [q.v.]

**The Case of Mr. George Edalji**
126. **1907.** Blake & Co; wrappers [reprint of articles published in the Daily Telegraph]
*see also* **The Story of Mr. George Edalji** [q.v. items 830 & 1013]

**The Case of Oscar Slater, Condemned for Murder in 1909 and Now in Penal Servitude**
127. **[1910?]** Wrappers; 80 pp. [first ed?]
128. **[1912]**. Hodder & Stoughton; first ed; illus; 99 pp; printed wrappers; 12 mo. (6x4½ in.)
129. **[1912]**. Doran, N.Y; wrappers
130. **[1914]**. Hodder & Stoughton; third ed; new preface by author
*see also* **Famous Crimes, Mysteries & Romances** [q.v. item 1013]

*THE CASE-BOOK OF SHERLOCK HOLMES
131. **[1927]**. Murray; first ed; red cloth, ruled borders in blind, titled gilt on front cover & spine; 320 pp; Cr. 8vo
132. **[1927]**. Doran, N.Y; first U.S. ed; light-brown cloth, titled in red; 320 pp; Cr. 8vo
133. **1929.** Murray; first Cheap Edition; brown cloth; 320 pp; Cr. 8vo

**The Case for Spirit Photography. By Sir Arthur Conan Doyle and Others**
134. **[1922]**. Hutchinson; first ed; illus; pale green wrappers printed in dark green; wrappers laid; 110 pp; Demy 8vo

**The Centurion**
135. **1922.** In: The Story-Teller, Dec. issue

***Charles Augustus Milverton [The Adventure of]**
136. **1904.** Story in: The Strand Magazine, Apr. issue; illus. by Sidney Paget
137. **1905.** Story in: The Return of Sherlock Holmes [q.v.]

**A Chat About Children, Snakes and Zebus**
138. **1918.** In: The Strand Magazine

**Christmas in Trouble**
139. **1922.** In: The Poems of Arthur Conan Doyle [q.v.]

**Christmas in Wartime**
140. **1919.** Poem in: The Guards Came Through [q.v.]

**The Club-footed Grocer [The Story of]**
141. **1898.** Story in: The Strand Magazine; illus. by Sidney Pagets
142. **1908.** In: Round The Fire Stories [q.v.]

**Collected Poems of Arthur Conan Doyle**
*see* **The Poems of Arthur Canon Doyle** [q.v.]

THE COMING OF THE FAIRIES
143. **[1922]**. Hodder & Stoughton; first ed; illus. from photographs; blue cloth, titled gilt on spine; 139 pp; Cr. 8vo
144. **[1922]**. Doran, N.Y; first U.S. ed; light-brown cloth titled in black (dark-brown?) with a photograph superimposed on front cover; black lettering on spine; 196 pp; 8vo
145. **[1924?]** Hodder & Stoughton; second ed. illus; 8vo
[Locke, p. 72: "An enlarged edition with fresh evidence and new photographs is on the eve of publication by The Psychic Press"]

**The Coming of the Huns**
146. **1911.** Story in: The Last Galley [q.v.]
147. **[1922]**. Story in: Tales of Long Ago [q.v.]

**Compensations**
148. **1911.** Poem in: Songs of the Road [q.v.]

**Comrades**
149. **1922.** In: The Poems of Arthur Conan Doyle [q.v.]

**The Confession**
150. **1900.** Short Story in: The Universal Magazine, vol. I, No. 2, Mar. issue; illus. with a photograph of the author and a drawing by H. White [not in Locke]

**The Contest**
151. **1911.** Story in: The Last Galley [q.v.]
152. **[1922].** Story in: Tales of Long Ago [q.v.]

***The Copper Beeches [The Adventure of]**
153. **1892.** Story in: The Strand Magazine, Jun. issue; illus. by Sidney Paget
154. **1892.** Story in: The Adventures of Sherlock Holmes [q.v.]

**Corporal Dick's Promotion**
155. **1887.** Poem in: The Boy's Own Paper
156. **1898.** Poem in: Songs of Action [q.v.]

**Coup d'oeuil sur la guerre**
157. **[1909].** Hutchinson: 19 pp.

**Crabbe's Practice**
158. **1884.** Story in: The Boy's Own Paper [published anonymously]

***The Creeping Man [The Adventure of]**
159. **1923.** Story in: The Strand Magazine, Jul. issue; illus. by Sidney Paget
160. **1927.** Story in: The Case-Book of Sherlock Holmes [q.v.]

**Cremona — A Ballad of the Irish Brigade**
161. **1898.** Poem in: The Cornhill Magazine, Jan. issue
162. **1898.** Poem in: Songs of Action [q.v.]
163. **1914.** Poem in: Modern Anglo-Irish Verse [q.v. item 1024]

**The Crime of the Brigadier [Or How the Brigadier Slew the Fox]**
164. **1900.** Story in: The Strand Magazine; illus. by W. B. Wollen
165. **1900.** Story in: The Green Flag [q.v.]
166. **1903.** Story in: Adventures of Gerard [q.v.]
167. **[n.d.].** Story in: The Great Shadow and Other Napoleonic Tales [q.v.]

**The Crime of the Congo**
168. **[1909].** Hutchinson; first ed; frontis; black and white paper boards with photograph on front cover; maroon cloth spine; 128 pp; 8vo
169. **[1909].** As above; variant binding in pic. wrappers
170. **1909.** Doubleday, Page & Co; N.Y.; first U.S. ed; buff cloth, lettered on front cover & spine; 8vo
(Translated into French and German)

***The Crooked Man [The Adventure of]**
171. **1893.** Story in: The Strand Magazine, Jul. issue; illus. by Sidney Paget
172. **1894.** Story in: The Memoirs of Sherlock Holmes [q.v.]
173. **[1947].** Story in: The Great Detectives [q.v. item 1018]

***The Crown Diamond: An Evening with Sherlock Holmes — A Play in One Act**
174. **1921.** Performed, but unpublished
175. **1958.** Privately printed by the Baskerrette Press, N.Y.; for subscribers only; cloth-backed boards, paper label; limited to 59 copies

**The Croxley Master: A Great Tale of the Prize Ring**
176. **1899.** Story in: The Strand Magazine, Oct.-Dec. issues; illus. by Sidney Paget
177. **1900.** Story in: The Green Flag [q.v.]
178. **1907.** McClure, Philips, N.Y; first ed. in book form; col. frontis; light-brown cloth, with picture of two pugilists superimposed on front cover; 76 pp; 8vo

**The Croxley Master and Other Stories of Ring and Camp**
179. **1909.** George H. Doran, N.Y; 8vo

**The Curse of Eve**
180. **[?].** Story in: The Idler Magazine
181. **1894.** Story in: Round The Red Lamp [q.v.]

**Cyprian Overbeck Wells**
*see* **A Literary Mosaic**

***The Dancing Men [The Adventure of]**
182. **1903.** Story in: The Strand Magazine, Dec. issue; illus. by Sidney Paget
182B. **1905.** Story in: The Return of Sherlock Holmes [q.v.]

**DANGER! [And Other Stories]**
183. **1914.** Story in: The Strand Magazine, Jul. issue; illus. by E. S. Hodgson
184. **1918.** Murray; first ed; fine red diaper-grain cloth, titled on front cover in blind; spine gilt; 246 pp; Cr. 8vo
185. **1918.** As above, variant binding in light-brown fine-grain cloth, ruled border & titling on front cover in black; Cr. 8vo [not in Locke]
186. **1918.** Murray; first ed; Colonial Library issue; beige cloth, pic. blocked in dark-blue; Cr. 8vo.
187. **[n.d.].** Doran, N.Y; first U.S. ed.

**Darkness**
188. **1911.** Poem in: Songs of the Road [q.v.]

**The Dealings of Captain Sharkey and Other Tales of Pirates**
189. **[1919?].** Doran, N.Y; red morocco-grain cloth, dec. in blind, gilt; pic. d.w.
190. **[n.d.]** Murray

**The Debatable Case of Mrs. Emsley**
*see* **Strange Studies from Life [q.v.]**

**Debate with Dr. Joseph McCabe**
*see* **The Truth of Spiritualism [q.v.]**

**[The Debut of] Bimbashi Joyce**
191. **1897.** In: Punch
192. **1900.** In: The Green Flag [q.v.]
193. [*c.* **1919**]. In: Princess Mary's Gift Book [q.v. item 1033]

**December's Snow**
194. **1911.** Poem in: Songs of the Road [q.v.]

**"De Profundis"**
195. **1892.** In: The Idler Magazine, Mar. issue
196. **1894.** In: McClure's Magazine, Nov. issue
197. **1911.** Story in: The Last Galley [q.v.]

A DESERT DRAMA
198. **1898.** U.S. ed. of The Tragedy of the Korosko [q.v.]

***The Devil's Foot [The Adventure of]**
199. **1910.** Story in: The Strand Magazine, Dec. issue; illus. by Gilbert Holiday
200. **1917.** Story in: His Last Bow [q.v.]

***The Devil's Foot and Other Tales of Sherlock Holmes**
201. **[1921]**. Newnes' Sevenpenny Novels, No. 31; 128 pp; Sm. 8vo.

***The Disappearance of Lady Frances Carfax**
202. **1911.** Story in: The Strand Magazine, Dec. issue; illus. by Alec Ball
203. **1917.** Story in: His Last Bow [q.v.]

**The Disintegration Machine**
204. **1952.** Story in: The Professor Challenger Stories Omnibus [q.v.]

**Divorce Law Reform**
205. **1909.** The Divorce Law Reform Union; wrappers [not in Locke]
206. **1911.** Interview on this subject with Arthur Conan Doyle in: The Strand Magazine, Sep. issue [not in Locke]

**The Doctors of Hoyland**
207. **1894.** In: The Idler Magazine, Apr. issue
208. **1894.** In: McClure's Magazine, Aug. issue
209. **1894.** Story in: Round The Red Lamp [q.v.]

**The Doings of Raffles Haw**
210. **1892.** Cassell; first ed; dark-blue cloth, gilt lettering on spine; 256 pp; Cr. 8vo (reprinted: 1893; 1894; 1895; 1896; 1899; 1903; 1908)
211. **1909.** Cassell; New Edition; frontis; blue cloth dec. in black; gilt lettered; 256 pp; Cr. 8vo (reprinted 1912)
212. **1910.** Cassell's Sixpenny Novels; 128 pp; Sm. 8vo
213. **1910.** Cassell's Popular Edition (reprinted same year)

**The Doings of Raffles Haw with The Surgeon of Gaster Fell**
214. **[n.d.]**. Lupton, N.Y; The Armchair Library, No. 131; wrappers [pirated?]
*see also* **The Surgeon of Gaster Fell** [q.v.]

**The Dreamers**
215. **1928.** Story in: The Strand Magazine

DREAMLAND AND GHOSTLAND. **An Original Collection of Tales and Warnings from the Borderland of Substance and Shadow**
216. **[1886]**. Redway; red cloth dec. in black, titled on spine in gilt; 3 vols. 8vo [not in Locke]

**The Duello in France**
217. **1890.** In: The Cornhill Magazine, Dec. issue

A DUET WITH AN OCCASIONAL CHORUS
218. **1899.** Grant Richards; first ed; dark-green cloth, front cover and spine titled in gilt; 330 pp; 14 pp. adverts at end [Locke, p. 49: "one sheet of advertisements at end."] Cr. 8vo
219. **1899.** Grant Richards; First Cheap Edition (issued at the same time as the First Edition); red paper wrappers, lettered black; contents identical to First Ed; Cr. 8vo
220. **1899.** Appleton, N.Y; first U.S. ed; red buckram, dec. & titled gilt and silver; Cr. 8vo
221. **[1909]**. Newnes' Sixpenny Copyright Novels; 130 pp; Sm. 8vo
222. **1910.** Smith, Elder; tenth ed; Newly Revised; 342 pp; 8vo
223. **[n.d.]** Canadian Copyright Edition
224. **[n.d.]** Hodder & Stoughton Sevenpenny Library; Sm. 8vo

**A Duet — A Play**
225. **1903.** Adaptation of the novel; performed but unpublished
226. **[n.d.]**. Lacy's Acting Edition of Plays; 15 pp; wrappers

**A Duet**
227. **1902.** Nordon, p. 180, has it that Doyle wrote a short novel called: 'A Duet' in this year [a shortened version of his earlier work?]

***The Dying Detective [The Adventure of]**
228. **1913.** Story in: The Strand Magazine, Dec. issue; illus. by Wal Paget
229. **1917.** Story in: His Last Bow [q.v.]

**The Dying Whip**
230. **1898.** Poem in: Songs of Action [q.v.]

**The Early Christian Church and Modern Spiritualism**
231. **[1925]**. Psychic Press and Bookshop; wrappers; 11 pp; 8vo

**The Echo**
232. **1911.** Poem in: Songs of the Road [q.v.]

**Edgar Allan Poe Shrine, The Old House**
233. **1923.** The Shrine, Richmond, Va; U.S.A; first ed. [not in Locke]

**The Edge of the Unknown**
234. **1930.** Murray; 332 pp; 8vo

**The Empire — 1902**
235. **1911.** Poem in: Songs of the Road [q.v.]

**Empire Builders**
236. **1911.** Poem in: Songs of the Road [q.v.]

***The Empty House [The Adventure of]**
237. **1903.** Story in: The Strand Magazine, Oct. issue; illus. by Sidney Paget
238. **1905.** Story in: The Return of Sherlock Holmes [q.v.]

***The Empty House and Other Tales**
239. **[1921].** Newnes' Sevenpenny Library, No. 33; 128 pp; Sm. 8vo

**The End**
240. **1911.** Poem in: Songs of the Road [q.v.]

**The End of Devil Hawker**
241. **1930.** Story in: The Strand Magazine, Nov. issue

***The Engineer's Thumb [The Adventure of]**
242. **1892.** Story in: The Strand Magazine, Mar. issue; illus. by Sidney Paget
243. **1892.** Story in: The Adventures of Sherlock Holmes [q.v.]

**England and The Next War**
*see* **Great Britain and The Next War**

**The Evidence for Fairies**
244. **1921.** In: The Strand Magazine, Mar. issue
245. **1921.** George H. Doran, N.Y; first ed.

**An Exciting Christmas Eve**
246. **1887.** Story in: The Boy's Own Paper

THE EXPLOITS OF BRIGADIER GERARD
247. **1895.** In: The Strand Magazine; illus. by W. B. Wollen (serialised)
248. **1896.** Newnes; first ed; first issue; 24 illus. by W. B. Wollen; red fine-ribbed cloth, dec. with a sabre, etc. in black on front cover; titled gilt on front cover and spine; 'Strand Library' motif in black on back cover; 334 pp; adverts at end, dated 30.11.95; Cr. 8vo
249. **1896.** Newnes; first ed; second issue; identical to first ed. but with 8 pp. adverts at end, dated 10.2.96; Cr. 8vo
250. **1899.** Newnes; 24 illus. by W. B. Wollen; red cloth, 'Strand Library' motif in black on front cover; titled black & gilt; spine titled gilt; 334 pp; Sm. 8vo
251. **1932.** In: The Conan Doyle Historical Romances Omnibus, vol. II [q.v.]
252. **1956.** In: The Complete Napoleonic Stories Omnibus [q.v.]
253. **[n.d.].** Nelson; frontis. by Lionel Edwards; red cloth, dec. in blind, gilt; 8vo
254. **1976.** Murray; Introduction by Fitzroy Maclean; first ed. thus; 8vo

**Fairies Photographed. [An Epoch-making Event Described by A. Conan Doyle]**
255. **1920.** In: The Strand Magazine
256. **1921.** George H. Doran, N.Y; first printing in book form
*see also* **The Evidence for Fairies**

**The Fall of Lord Barrymore**
257. **1912.** Story in: The Strand Magazine; illus. by H. M. Brock
258. **1918.** In: Danger! And Other Stories [q.v.]

**A False Start**
259. **1894.** Story in Round The Red Lamp [q.v.]

**The Farewell**
260. **1922.** In: The Poems of Arthur Conan Doyle [q.v.]

**The Farnshire Cup**
261. **1898.** Poem in: Songs of Action [q.v.]

**Fate**
262. **1919.** Poem in: The Guards Came Through [q.v.]

**The Fate of the Evangeline**
263. **1885.** Story in: The Boy's Own Paper

**The Fiend of the Cooperage**
264. **1908.** Story in: Round The Red Lamp [q.v.]

***The Final Problem [The Adventure of]**
265. **1893.** Story in: The Strand Magazine, Dec. issue; illus. by Sidney Paget
266. **1894.** Story in: The Memoirs of Sherlock Holmes [q.v.]

**The Fires of Fate**
267. **1909.** Dramatisation of *The Tragedy of the Korosko;* performed, but unpublished

THE FIRM OF GIRDLESTONE. **A Romance of the Unromantic**
268. **1890.** Chatto & Windus; first ed; dark red-brown cloth; black design and lettering on front cover; gilt lettering and design on spine; 399 pp; 32 pp. adverts at end, dated April 1890; 8vo
269. **1892.** Chatto & Windus; scarlet fine diaper-grain cloth, ruled borders in blind; titled gilt; Cr. 8vo
270. **1893.** Tauchnitz Copyright Edition, Leipzig; paper wrappers; 2 vols; vol. I: 272 pp; adverts at end, dated 1893; vol. II: 270 pp; adverts at end, dated 1893; Sm. 8vo
271. [*c.* **1896].** Fenno, N.Y; light-blue cloth, front cover & spine dec. & titled white; Cr. 8vo
272. **1923.** Murray's Fiction Library; blue boards; front cover dec. in blind; spine dec. & titled gilt; 399 pp; 1 p. advert at end; Sm. 8vo

273. **[n.d.].** Collins; Modern Fiction Clear Type Press; col. frontis. by Lex De Renault; pic. title-page by Chas. Pears; light-blue fine-ribbed cloth, dec. & titled in blind; gilt; Sm. 8vo
274. **[n.d.].** As above, variant binding in green
275. **[n.d.].** Lupton Pub. Co; N.Y; frontis; red fine-ribbed cloth, ruled border in blind, gilt; t.e.g; Cr. 8vo

**The First Cargo**
276. **1911.** Story in: The Last Galley [q.v.]
277. **[1922].** Story in: Tales of Long Ago [q.v.]

***The Five Orange Pips**
278. **1891.** Story in: The Strand Magazine, Nov. issue; illus. by Sidney Paget
279. **1892.** Story in: The Adventures of Sherlock Holmes [q.v.]

**The Flag**
280. **[1908].** The Daily Mail for The Union Jack Club; first ed; pigskin over rounded-cornered boards, elaborately dec. in red inlay (the intials of the club) & gilt; t.e.g; bound by Sangorski & Sutcliffe for the publishers in a limited ed. of 150; Roy 4to (contains: The Grey Dress [q.v.])

**The Forbidden Subject**
281. **1923.** In: The Strand Magazine, Aug. issue
282. **1923.** In: Three of Them [q.v.]

**A Foreign Office Romance**
283. **1894.** In: McClure's Magazine, Dec. issue
284. **1900.** Story in: The Green Flag [q.v.]

**A Forgotten Tale**
285. **1898.** Poem in: Songs of Action [q.v.]

**The Franklin's Maid**
286. **1898.** Poem in: Songs of Action [q.v.]

**The Frontier Line**
287. **1898.** Poem in: Songs of Action [q.v.]

**The Geographical Distribution of British Intellect**
288. **1888.** In: The Nineteenth Century, Aug. issue

**The German War, Some Sidelights and Reflections**
289. **1914.** Hodder & Stoughton; blue pic. printed wrappers lettered in black and red on front cover & spine; 8vo (most of the essays in this volume appeared originally in *The Fortnightly Review* and *The Daily Chronicle*)

**Giant Maximin**
290. **1911.** Story in: A Literary Pageant (periodical)
291. **[1922].** Story in: Tales of Long Ago [q.v.]

**The Glamour of the Arctic**
292. **1892.** In: The Idler Magazine, Jul. issue
293. **1894.** In: McClure's Magazine, Mar. issue

**A Glimpse of the Army**
294. **1900.** In: The Strand Magazine

***The 'Gloria Scott' [The Adventure of]**
295. **1893.** Story in: The Strand Magazine, Apr. issue; illus. by Sidney Paget
296. **1894.** Story in: The Memoirs of Sherlock Holmes [q.v.]

***The Golden Pince-nez [The Adventure of]**
297. **1904.** Story in: The Strand Magazine, Jul. issue; illus. by Sidney Paget
298. **1905.** Story in: The Return of Sherlock Holmes [q.v.]

**The Governor of St. Kitts**
299. **1897.** In: McClure's Magazine, May issue
300. **1922.** Story in: Tales of Pirates [q.v.]

THE GREAT BOER WAR
301. [?]. First appearance in: The Sphere; illus. by Sidney Paget
302. **1900.** Smith, Elder; first ed; blue fine-ribbed cloth ruled in blind, gilt; 552 pp; 5 folding maps and index; 10 pp. adverts at end; Large Cr. 8vo
303. **1901.** Smith, Elder; 13th impr; 680 pp.
304. **1902.** Smith, Elder; Complete Edition; 769 pp.
305. **[1903].** Nelson; Preface to the 'Final Edition', dated 1903; 7 illus; blue diaper-grain cloth, dec. with heavy ornamental borders in darker blue; spine titled gilt; t.e.g; 8vo

GREAT BRITAIN AND THE NEXT WAR
306. **1913.** In: The Fortnightly Review, Feb. issue, under the title of: 'England and The Next War'
307. **1914.** Small, Maynard, Boston; red boards, dec. & titled black; 48 pp; Cr. 8vo

**The Great Brown Pericord Motor**
308. **1905.** In: The Pictorial Magazine, Jan. issue

**The Great Keinplatz Experiment [and Other Stories]**
309. **1886.** Story in: Dreamland and Ghostland, vol. III [q.v.]
310. **1890.** Story in: The Captain of the Pole-Star and Other Tales [q.v.]
311. **[1894].** Rand, McNally, N.Y; first ed; red buckram, ruled borders, dec. & titled in gilt; t.e.g.; 8vo

**The Great Shadow**
312. **1892.** First appearance in Arrowsmith's Christmas Annual; pic. wrappers; 184 pp; Large 12mo [scarce in fine condition]
313. **1893.** Harper & Bros; N.Y; olive-green cloth, dec. & titled in red; Cr. 8vo

**The Great Shadow & Beyond The City**
314. **[1893].** Arrowsmith, Bristol; first illus. ed. by James Greig & Paul Hardy; brown cloth, dec. & titled in black & blue; spine gilt; Cr. 8vo
315. [*c.* **1893**]. Tauchnitz Copyright Edition, Leipzig; Sm. 8vo
316. **[1914].** Newnes' Sixpenny Copyright Novels; 128 pp; Sm. 8vo
317. **1956.** In: The Complete Napoleonic Stories Omnibus [q.v.]

**The Great Shadow and Other Napoleonic Tales**
318. **[n.d.].** Nelson's Copyright Novels; frontis; 344 pp; 40 pp. adverts at end; Sm. 8vo

***The Greek Interpreter [The Adventure of]**
319. **1893.** Story in: The Strand Magazine, Sept. issue; illus. by Sidney Paget
320. **1894.** Story in: The Memoirs of Sherlock Holmes [q.v.]

THE GREEN FLAG **[and Other Stories of War and Sport]**
321. **1893.** In: The Pall Mall Magazine, Jun. issue
322. **1900.** Smith, Elder; first ed; frontis; red cloth, pic. blocked in black & titled gilt on front cover & spine; 348 pp; 4 pp. adverts at end; Cr. 8vo
323. **1900.** McClure, Phillips, N.Y; first U.S. ed; green cloth, pic. blocked & titled in black, white, blue and gilt; Cr. 8vo
324. **1902.** Newnes; 130 pp; 8vo
325. [*c.* **1906**]. Smith, Elder; New and Cheaper Edition; frontis; Cr 8vo
326. **[n.d.].** Hodder & Stoughton's Sevenpenny Library; frontis; 256 pp; Sm. Cr. 8vo

**The Grey Dress**
327. **[1908].** Story in: The Flag [q.v.]

**The Groom's Encore**
328. **1911.** Poem in: Songs of the Road [q.v.]

**The Groom's Story**
329. **1898.** Poem in: The Cornhill Magazine, Apr. issue
330. **1898.** Poem in: Songs of Action [q.v.]

**Grousing**
331. **1919.** Poem in: The Guards Came Through [q.v.]

THE GUARDS CAME THROUGH AND OTHER POEMS
332. **1919.** Murray; first ed; red wrappers printed black; 78 pp; 2 pp. adverts at end; Sm 8vo (Most of the poems in this volume appear later in *The Poems of Arthur Conan Doyle* [q.v.])

**The Gully of Bluemansdyke**
333. **1881.** Story in: London Society Extra Christmas Number; illus; col. printed wrappers
334. **[1889].** Story in: Mysteries and Adventures [q.v.]
335. **[1889].** Story in: My Friend The Murderer and Other Mysteries and Adventures [q.v.]

THE GULLY OF BLUEMANSDYKE AND OTHER STORIES
336. **1893.** Walter Scott; first ed; maroon and green cloth, lettered in gilt; spine gilt; 8vo [scarce]
337. **[1893].** Walter Scott, second ed; pic. wrappers; 8vo
(This book first appeared under the title of 'Mysteries and Adventures')

**The Guns in Sussex**
338. **1919.** Poem in: The Guards Came Through [q.v.]

**Haig is Moving**
339. **1919.** Poem in: The Guards Came Through [q.v.]

**Halves [or Brothers] — A Play**
340. **1889.** Adapted from a novel entitled: 'Halves' by James Payn; performed, but unpublished

**The Haunted Grange of Goresthorpe**
341. [*c.* **1879**]. Unpublished

**My First Operation**
342. **1894.** Story in: Round The Red Lamp [q.v.]

***His Last Bow**
343. **1917.** Story in: The Strand Magazine, Sep. issue. illus. by A. Gilbert
344. **1917.** Last story in: His Last Bow [q.v.]

*HIS LAST BOW. **Some Reminiscences of Sherlock Holmes**
345. **1917.** Murray; first ed; red cloth, titled gilt front cover & spine; 305 pp; 6 pp. adverts at end; Cr. 8vo
346. **[1917].** Doran, N.Y; first U.S. ed; pink cloth, titled in black; Cr. 8vo
347. **[n.d.].** Newnes; pic. wrappers by Frank Wrig; Cr 8vo
348. **1971.** Murray; paperback; pic. cover; 205 pp; 8vo

THE HISTORY OF SPIRITUALISM
349. **1926.** Cassell; first ed; 16 illus; blue cloth, gilt lettered; d.w; 2 vols; Roy 4to
350. **1926.** Doran, N.Y; first U.S. ed.

HISTORY OF THE GREAT WAR: THE BRITISH CAMPAIGNS
351. **1917-20.** Doran, N.Y; first U.S. ed; cloth; maps; 6 vols. [This is the American edition of The British Campaigns in France and Flanders — not in Locke]

**A History of the Irish Brigade in the Service of France**
352. **1954.** First appearance in: The Irish Times

**H.M.S. Foudroyant**
353. **1898.** Poem in: Songs of Action [q.v.]

**The Holocaust of Manor Place**
*see* **Strange Studies from Life** [q.v.]

**The Home-coming**
354. **1909.** Story in: The Strand Magazine, Dec. issue; illus. by Arthur Twidle
355. **1911.** Story in: The Last Galley [q.v.]
356. **[1922].** Story in: Tales of Long Ago [q.v.]

**The Home-coming of the "Euridice"**
357. **1898.** Poem in: Songs of Action [q.v.]

**Hope**
358. **1911.** Poem in: Songs of the Road [q.v.]

**The Horror of the Heights**
359. **1913.** Story in: The Strand Magazine; illus. by W. R. S. Stott
360. **1918.** Story in: Danger! And Other Stories [q.v.]

**Houdini — An Enigma**
361. **1927.** In: The Strand Magazine

*THE HOUND OF THE BASKERVILLES
362. **1901-2.** In: The Strand Magazine; illus. by Sidney Paget (serialised)
363. **1902.** Newnes; first ed; first issue; 16 illus. by Sidney Paget; scarlet cloth, pic. blocked & titled in black & gilt; 359 pp; Cr. 8vo (misprint "you" for "yours", p. 13, line 3)
364. **1902.** McClure, Phillips, N.Y; first U.S. ed; 8 illus. by Sidney Paget (only 2 of which appear in the first English ed.); red cloth, lettered in white on front cover & spine; 249 pp; 4 pp. adverts at end; Cr. 8vo
365. **1902.** Grosset & Dunlap, N.Y; 4th impr; 8 illus. by Sidney Paget; red cloth, lettered in white on front cover & spine; 249 pp; no adverts at end; Cr. 8vo (At head of title: 'A Special Limited Edition')
366. **[1912].** Newnes' Sixpenny Copyright Novels; 126 pp; Sm. 8vo
367. **1918.** Murray; fourth impr; 8vo
368. **[1932].** Newnes; reprint; dark-blue cloth, pic. blocked with 3 saplings & foliage in blind, gilt; pic. d.w. by Shilton; 8vo
369. **1939.** Murray; Cheaper Edition (2/-); light-blue cloth, author's facsimile signature in darker blue on front cover; spine titled blue; pic. d.w; Sm. 8vo

**The House of Temperley**
370. **1910.** A play written for Henry Irving in 1895, performed, but not published till 1910. [Locke dates it as 1912 and calls it 'a dramatized version of Rodney Stone'; it has since been declared as only 'after' that novel]

**How Brigadier Gerard Lost His Ear**
371. **1902.** Story in: The Strand Magazine; illus. by W. B. Wollen
372. **[1903].** Story in: Adventures of Gerard [q.v.]

**How Etienne Gerard said Goodbye to his Master**
373. **1903.** Story in: The Strand Magazine; illus. by W. B. Wollen
374. **[1903].** In: Adventures of Gerard [q.v.] under the title of: *The Last Adventure of the Brigadier*

**How It Happened**
375. **1913.** In: The Strand Magazine; illus. by Cyrus Cuneo
376. **1918.** In: Danger! And Other Stories

**How the Brigadier Came to the Castle of Gloom**
377. **1895.** Story in: The Strand Magazine, Jul. issue; illus. by W. B. Wollen
378. **1896.** Story in: The Exploits of Brigadier Gerard [q.v.]

**How the Brigadier Captured Saragossa**
*see* **How the Brigadier Joined the Hussars of Conflans**

**How the Brigadier Held the King**
379. **1895.** Story in: The Strand Magazine, Apr. issue; illus. by W. B. Wollen
380. **1896.** Story in: The Exploits of Brigadier Gerard [q.v.]

**How the Brigadier Joined the Hussars of Conflans**
381. **1903.** Story in: The Strand Magazines; illus. by W. B. Wollen
382. **[1903].** Story in: Adventures of Gerard [q.v.] under the title of: *How the Brigadier Captured Saragossa*

**How the Brigadier Played for a Kingdom**
383. **1895.** Story in: The Strand Magazine; illus. by W. B. Wollen
384. **1896.** Story in: The Exploits of Brigadier Gerard [q.v.]

**How the Brigadier Rode to Minsk**
385. **1902.** Story in: The Strand Magazine; illus. by W. B. Wollen
386. **[1903].** Story in: The Adventures of Gerard [q.v.]

**How the Brigadier Saved the Army**
387. **1902.** Story in: The Strand Magazine; illus. by W. B. Wollen
388. **[1903].** Story in: The Adventures of Gerard [q.v.]

**How the Brigadier Slew the Brothers of Ajaccio**
389. **1895.** Story in: The Strand Magazine, Jun. issue; illus. by W. B. Wollen
390. **1896.** Story in: The Exploits of Brigadier Gerard [q.v.]

**How the Brigadier Took the Field against the Marshal Millefleurs**
391. **1895.** Story in: The Strand Magazine, Aug. issue; illus. by W. B. Wollen
392. **1896.** Story in: The Exploits of Brigadier Gerard [q.v.]

**How the Brigadier was Tempted by the Devil**
393. **1895.** Story in: The Strand Magazine, Sep. issue; illus. by W. B. Wollen
394. **1896.** Story in: The Exploits of Brigadier Gerard [q.v.]

**How the King Held the Brigadier**
395. **1895.** Story in: The Strand Magazine, May issue; illus. by W. B. Wollen
396. **1896.** Story in: The Exploits of Brigadier Gerard [q.v.]

**A Hunting Morning**
397. **1898.** Poem in: Songs of Action [q.v.]
398. **1909.** Published by Sonnenschein; set to music by A. J. Silver

**A Hymn of Empire**
399. **1911.** Poem in: Songs of the Road [q.v.]

**An Iconoclast**
400. **1911.** Story in: The Last Galley [q.v.]
401. **[1922].** Story in: Tales of Long Ago [q.v.]

**If I Could Preach Just Once**
402. [*c*. **1923**]. An article [not in Locke]

***The Illustrious Client [The Adventure of]**
403. **1925.** Story in: The Strand Magazine, Feb. issue; illus. by Howard K. Elcock [not in Locke]
404. **1927.** Story in: The Case-Book of Sherlock Holmes [q.v.]

**The Immortal Memory**
405. **1901.** Mitchell & Sons, Edinburgh; wrappers [extracts from Doyle's lecture given 23 Mar. 1901 at the Balmoral Hotel, Edinburgh — not in Locke]

**An Incursion into Diplomacy**
406. **1906.** In: The Cornhill Magazine, Jun. issue

**Independant Testimony as to the Mediumship of Florence Cook**
407. **1926.** Psychic Bookshop [not in Locke]

**The Inner Room**
408. **1898.** Poem in: Songs of Action [q.v.]

**In Quest of Truth**
409. **1914.** Watts; 31 pp; wrappers (reprinted from the Rationalist Press Ass. Ltd.)

**The Irish Colonel**
410. **1898.** Poem in: Songs of Action [q.v.]
411. **1914.** In: Modern Anglo-Irish Poets [q.v.]

**Is Sir Oliver Lodge Right? Yes!**
412. **1917.** Article in: The Strand Magazine

**Jane Annie, or, The Good-Conduct Prize. By J. M. Barrie and A. C. Doyle**
413. **1893.** Chappell & Co; A comic opera, with music by Ernest Ford

**The Japanned Box [The Story of]**
414. **1899.** Story in: The Strand Magazine; illus. by Sidney Paget
415. **1908.** In: Round The Fire Stories [q.v.]

**Jelland's Voyage**
416. **1892.** Story in: Phil May's Illustrated Winter Annual [not in Locke]
417. **1908.** Story in: Round the Fire Stories [q.v.]

**The Jew's Breastplate [The Story of]**
418. **1899.** Story in: The Strand Magazine; illus. by Sidney Paget
419. **1908.** In: Round The Fire Stories [q.v.]

**J. Habakuk Jephson's Statement**
420. **1884.** Story in: The Cornhill Magazine, Jan. issue
421. **1886.** Story in: Dreamland and Ghostland, vol. I [q.v.]
422. **[1891].** In: Strange Stories of Coincidence & Ghostly Adventure [q.v. item 1040]

**John Barrington Cowles**
423. **1886.** Story in: Dreamland and Ghostland, vol. III [q.v.]

**John Huxford's Hiatus**
424. **1888.** Story in: The Cornhill Magazine, Jun. issue
425. **1890.** Story in: The Captain of the Pole-Star [q.v.]
426. [*c*. **1892**]. Story in: The Sign of the Four. A Scandal in Bohemia — And Other Stories [q.v.]

**The Journey — A poetical one-act play**
427. **1922.** In: The Poems of Arthur Conan Doyle [q.v.]

**The King of the Foxes**
428. **1898.** Story in: The Windsor Magazine; illus by H. G. Jalland
429. **1900.** Story in: The Green Flag [q.v.]

THE LAND OF MIST
430. **1925-6.** In: The Strand Magazine; illus. by F. E. Hiley (serialised)
431. **[1926].** Hutchinson: first ed; first issue; dark-green cloth, dec. & titled in blind and light-blue-green on cover & spine; 294 pp; 24 pp. cat. at end, dated Spring 1926, and 1p. ad relating to psychic works; Cr. 8vo
432. **[1926].** Hutchinson; first ed; second issue; red boards, double-ruled borders & medallion in blind, titled black; 1 p. ad relating to psychic works, but no catalogue; Cr. 8vo
433. **[1926].** Doran, N.Y; first U.S. ed; pale olive-green cloth, ruled & titled in dark-green; Cr. 8vo
434. **[n.d.].** The Universal Library Co; orange boards, ruled borders & spine titled in black; pic. d.w. (subtitled '13th Thou.); Cr. 8vo
435. **1952.** In: The Professor Challenger Stories Omnibus [q.v.]

**The Last Adventure of the Brigadier**
*see* **How Etienne Gerard said Good-bye to his Master**

*THE LAST ADVENTURES OF SHERLOCK HOLMES
436. **1902.** Newnes; Souvenir Edition; 25 illus. by Sidney Paget; dark-blue cloth, pic. blocked and titled gilt, front cover & spine; publisher's device in blind on back cover; 296 pp; t.e.g; Cr. 8vo (A re-issue of The Memoirs of Sherlock Holmes [q.v.])
437. **1906.** The above, reprinted under the title of 'The Memoirs of Sherlock Holmes' [q.v.]

THE LAST GALLEY. **[Impressions and Tales]**
438. **1911.** Smith, Elder; first ed; red cloth, pic. blocked & titled gilt; frontis. by N. C. Wyeth and one other illus; 298 pp; 14 pp. cat. at end; 8vo
439. **1911.** Bell; Indian & Colonial Library Edition; first ed. thus; light-blue cloth heavily blocked & titled in blind and gilt; 298 pp; Bell's cats. 14 pp. and 16 pp; dated Jan. 1911, at end; Cr. 8vo
440. **1912.** Smith, Elder; New Edition; red cloth, gilt lettering front cover & spine; (content identical to first ed.); Cr. 8vo
441. **[1914].** Newnes' Sixpenny Copyright Novels; Sm. 8vo
442. **[1922].** Story in: Tales of Long Ago [q.v.]

**The Last of the Legions [And Other Tales of Long Ago]**
443. **1911.** Story in: The Last Galley [q.v.]
444. **1922.** Doran, N.Y; first ed.
445. **[1922].** Story in: Tales of Long Ago [q.v.]

**The Latin Tutor [The Story of]**
446. **1899.** Story in: The Strand Magazine; illus. by Sidney Paget
447. **1908.** In: Round The Fire Stories [q.v.] under the title of: *The Usher of Lea House School, or The Latin Tutor*

**The Law of the Ghost**
448. **1919.** In: The Strand Magazine

**A Lay of the Links**
449. **1898.** Poem in: Songs of Action ]q.v.]

**The Leather Funnel**
450. **1903.** Story in: The Strand Magazine
451. **1908.** Story in: Round The Fire Stories [q.v.]

**The Leather-Skin Tribe**
452. **1918.** In: The Strand Magazine
453. **1918.** In: Danger! And Other Stories [q.v.]
454. **1923.** In: Three of Them [q.v.]

**Life and Death in the Blood**
455. **1883.** In: Good Words (periodical)

**Life on a Greenland Whaler**
456. **1897.** In: The Strand Magazine; illus. from photographs

**The Lift**
457. **1922.** Story in: The Strand Magazine, Jun. issue [not in Locke]

**A Lilt of the Road**
458. **1911.** Poem in: Songs of the Road [q.v.]

**Lindisfaire**
459. **1919.** Poem in: The Guards Came Through [q.v.]

***The Lion's Mane [The Adventure of]**
460. **1926.** Story in: The Strand Magazine, Dec. issue; illus. by Howard K. Elcock
461. **1927.** Story in: The Case-Book of Sherlock Holmes [q.v.]

**A Literary Mosaic [or Cyprian Overbeck Wells]**
462. **1886.** In: The Boy's Own Paper
463. **1890.** In: The Captain of the Pole-Star and Other Tales [q.v.]

**Little Billy**
464. **1922.** In: The Poems of Arthur Conan Doyle [q.v.]

**Little Boy Love. A Song. Words by A. Conan Doyle; music by Maude Valerie White**
465. **[n.d.].** Published by Boosey [not in Locke]

**The Little Square Box**
466. **1881.** In: London Society Christmas Number [not in Locke]

**The Lord of Chateau Noir**
467. **1894.** Story in: The Strand Magazine: illus. by W. B. Wollen
468. **1900.** Story in: The Green Flag [q.v.]

**The Lord of Falconbridge**
469. **1909.** Story in: The Strand Magazine, Aug. issue; illus. by Arthur Twidle
470. **1911.** Story in: The Last Galley [q.v.]
471. **[1924].** In: Rosemary [q.v. item 1036]

**The Los Amigos Fiasco**
472. **1892.** Story in: The Idler Magazine, Dec. issue
473. **1894.** Story in: Round The Red Lamp [q.v.]

**The Lost Special [The Story of]**
474. **1898.** Story in: The Strand Magazine; illus. by Max Cowper
475. **1908.** In: Round The Fire Stories [q.v.]

THE LOST WORLD. **Being an Account of the Recent Amazing Adventures of Professor George E. Challenger, Lord John Roxton, Professor Summerlee & Mr. E. D. Malone of The Daily Gazette**
476. **[1912].** In: The Strand Magazine; illus. by Harry Rountree (serialised)
477. **[1912].** Hodder & Stoughton; first ed; 8 illus; blue cloth; front cover blocked in gilt with a portrait of George E. Challenger and ruled border and titling in white; spine titled in gilt; 369 pp; Cr. 8vo

478. **[1912].** Hodder & Stoughton; Edition-de-luxe; 13 illus. (inc. frontis.); some illus. in col; 2 maps; beige-brown cloth over bevelled boards, pic. blocked and titled in dark-brown; spine titled in dark-brown and gilt; top edges blue; illus. e.p.s; 319 pp; 4to
479. **[1912].** As above, variant binding in light-blue cloth; large gilt lettering and design in blind on front cover; spine lettered in gilt; 4to
480. **[1912].** Hodder & Stoughton — George H. Doran, N.Y; first U.S. ed; 16 illus. (nearly all differing from those in the English editions); buff fine-grain cloth, pic. blocked; front cover & spine gilt lettered; 309 pp; Cr. 8vo
481. **1952.** In: The Professor Challenger Stories Omnibus [q.v.]

**Lot No. 249**
482. **1894.** Story in: Harper's Magazine, Sep. issue [not in Locke]
482B. **1894.** Story in: Round The Red Lamp [q.v.]

**The Love Affair of George Vincent Parker**
*see* **Strange Studies from Life** [q.v.]

**The Man From Archangel**
483. **[1889].** Story in: Mysteries and Adventures [q.v.]
484. **[1889].** Story in: The Captain of the Pole-Star [q.v.]
485. [*c.* **1895].** Optimus Printing Co; N.Y; "Handy Classics" series of "Choice Stories by Famous Authors" No. 14; wrappers; 32 pp. [very scarce — not in Locke]
486. **1898.** Street & Smith, N.Y; first ed. in book form

**The Man From Archangel and Other Tales of Adventure**
487. **(n.d.).** Doran, N.Y; orange cloth, pic. blocked & titled in green; Cr. 8vo

***The Man with the Twisted Lip [The Adventure of]**
488. **1891.** Story in: The Strand Magazine, Dec. issue; illus. by Sidney Paget
489. **1892.** Story in: The Adventures of Sherlock Holmes [q.v.]
490. **[1921].** Newnes' Sevenpenny Novels, No. 32; 128 pp; Sm. 8vo

**The Man with the Watches [The Story of]**
491. **1898.** Story in: The Strand Magazine; illus. by Frank Craig
492. **1908.** In: Round The Fire Stories [q.v.]

**Man's Limitation**
493. **1911.** Poem in: Songs of the Road [q.v.]

THE MARACOT DEEP
494. **1927-8.** In: The Strand Magazine; illus. by Tom Peddie (serialised)
495. **1929.** Murray; first ed; 310 pp; 8vo
496. **1930.** Murray; first cheap ed; fine red diaper-grain cloth, front cover & spine titled gilt; 310 pp; 10 pp. adverts at end; Cr. 8vo
497. **[1930].** As above, variant binding in brown cloth, titled on front cover in blind; spine gilt; Cr. 8vo

**The Marriage of the Brigadier**
498. **1910.** Story in: The Strand Magazine. Sep. issue; illus. by Gilbert Holiday
499. **1911.** Story in: The Last Galley [q.v.]

**Master**
500. **1898.** Poem in: Songs of Action [q.v.]

***The Mazarin Stone [The Adventure of]**
501. **1921.** Story in: The Strand Magazine, Oct. issue; illus. by A. Gilbert
502. **1927.** Story in: The Case-Book of Sherlock Holmes [q.v.]

**The Medal of Brigadier Gerard**
503. **1894.** Story in: The Strand Magazine; illus. by W. B. Wollen
503B. **1896.** Story in: The Exploits of Brigadier Gerard [q.v.] under the title of: *How the Brigadier Won His Medal*

**A Medical Document**
504. **1894.** Story in: Round The Red Lamp [q.v.]

MEMORIES AND ADVENTURES **[Autobiography]**
505. **1923.** In: The Strand Magazine (serialised)
506. **[1924].** Hodder & Stoughton; first ed; 8 illus; blue cloth, gilt lettering on spine; 408 pp; Demy 8vo
507. **1924.** Little, Brown, Boston; first U.S. ed; illus; blue cloth, gilt; Demy 8vo
508. **1930.** Murray; Second Edition; 460 pp.

*THE MEMOIRS OF SHERLOCK HOLMES
509. **1894.** Newnes; first ed; 25 full-plate illus. by Sidney Paget, and one illus. in text; dark-blue cloth over bevelled boards; pic. blocked in black on front cover with 'Strand Library' motif; gilt lettering on spine; 4to [scarce in fine state]
510. **1894.** Harper & Bros; N.Y; first U.S. ed; illus. by W. H. Hyde and Sidney Paget; blue cloth; cloth slipcase; 281 pp; 8vo (Includes The Cardboard Box [q.v.]. Was withdrawn from circulation when Doyle discovered this fact, as it was contrary to his instructions to include this story) [very scarce]
511. **[1894].** Burt, N.Y; 4 illus; blue cloth, pic. blocked & titled in black & olive-brown; Cr. 8vo
512. **1906.** Newnes; Souvenir Edition; 25 illus. by Sidney Paget; dark-blue cloth, pic. blocked & titled gilt, front cover & spine; publisher's device in blind on back cover; 296 pp; t.e.g; Cr. 8vo

513. **1911.** Smith, Elder; Sixpenny Edition; frontis; blue cloth, dec. with a repeated motif in blind; gilt; 8vo
514. **1915.** Smith, Elder; New Edition; 25 illus. by Sidney Paget; red cloth, gilt lettered; 8vo
515. **1924.** Murray; first Thin Paper Edition; red fine-grain cloth; author's initials on front cover in gilt; spine dec. & titled in gilt; 248 pp; Sm. 8vo
516. **[n.d.].** Newnes; Cheap Edition; printed in double column; Cr. 8vo
*see also* **The Last Adventures of Sherlock Holmes** [q.v.]

**The Methods of R. L. Stevenson in Fiction**
517. **1890.** In: The National Review, Jan. issue [not in Locke]

MICAH CLARKE. **[His Statement]**
518. **1889.** Longmans, Green; first ed; dark-blue cloth over bevelled boards; lettered in gilt on front cover & spine; flowered e.p.s; t.e.g; 421 pp; 18 pp. adverts at end, dated June 1889; Cr. 8vo
519. **1889.** Longmans, Green; Second Edition — issued same month as first ed. (reprinted twice in this year)
520. **1890.** Longmans, Green; New Edition; frontis. & vignette title page; maroon cloth, blocked & titled silver on front cover; spine titled silver; 421 pp; 12 pp. adverts at end, dated Aug. 1889 (reprinted 1890 three times; 1891 once; 1892 once; 1896 once) [1892 ed. has 24 pp. cat. at end]
521. [*c.* **1893**]. Tauchnitz Copyright Edition, Leipzig; 2 vols; Sm. 8vo
522. **1896.** Longmans, Green; New Edition; maroon cloth, dec. & titled gilt; frontis., vignette title page and 8 illus. by HMP (H. M. Paget); Cr. 8vo (reprinted 1898)
523. [*c.* **1896**]. Fenno, N.Y; light-blue cloth; front cover & spine dec. & titled white; Cr 8vo
524. **1903.** Newnes; first Cheap Edition; 8 illus. by H. M. Brock
525. **1911.** Longmans, Green; School Edition; 6 illus. by H. M. Paget and 14 illus. by H. R. Millar; brown cloth; front cover pic. blocked and titled in dark-brown; spine titled dark-brown; floral e.p.s.; 216 pp; Cr. 8vo
526. **[n.d.].** H. M. Caldwell, N.Y; portrait frontis; red fine-ribbed cloth, ruled & dec. with a series of title insignia in blind & gilt; Cr. 8vo
527. **[n.d.]** Nelson's Copyright Library; frontis. & vignette title page; red cloth; spine titled gilt; 560 pp; 16 pp. adverts at end; Sm. 8vo
528. **1931.** In: The Conan Doyle Historical Romances Omnibus [q.v.]

**A Midshipman's Story**
529. **1885.** In: Cassell's Magazine, Dec. issue

**The Military Lessons of the War. A Rejoinder**
530. **1901.** In: The Cornhill Magazine, Jan. issue

**Mind and Matter**
531. **1911.** Poem in Songs of the Road [q.v.]

**Miracle Town. Wonders of a Monster Munitions Settlement**
532. **1916.** In: The Daily Graphic, Tues. Nov. 28th [not in Locke]

***The Missing Three-Quarter [The Adventure of]**
533. **1904.** Story in: The Strand Magazine, Aug. issue; illus. by Sidney Paget
534. **1904.** Story in: The Return of Sherlock Holmes [q.v.]

**Multiple Reviewing**
535. **1899.** In: The Bookman, Jul. issue [not in Locke]

***The Musgrave Ritual [The Adventure of]**
536. **1893.** Story in: The Strand Magazine, May issue; illus. by Sidney Paget
537. **1894.** Story in: The Memoirs of Sherlock Holmes [q.v.]

**My Favourite Novelist and His Best Book**
538. **1900.** Munsey's Magazine, Mar. issue [not in Locke]

**My First Book: Juvenilia**
539. **1893.** In: The Idler Magazine, Jan. issue
540. **1894.** In: McClure's Magazine, Aug. issue
*see also* **My First Book** [q.v. item 1025]

**My Friend The Murderer [And Other Mysteries and Adventures]**
541. **1882.** Story in: London Society Extra Christmas Number
542. **[1889].** Story in: Mysteries and Adventures [q.v.]
543. [*c.* **1890**]. H. M. Caldwell, N.Y; frontis. portrait of the author; illus. by J. W. K; buff cloth, the front cover dec. in the style of a Persian carpet in maroon, green and gilt; spine similarly decorated; dec. title page, printed in red & blue; 12 mo (6 x 4¾ in.)
544. [*c.* **1892**]. In: The Sign of Four. A Scandal in Bohemia — And Other Stories [q.v.]
545. [*c.* **1890**]. M. A. Donahue, Chicago; 8vo
546. **1893.** Lovell, Coryell [Higham, p. 354, states this to be the first printing]

THE MYSTERY OF CLOOMBER
547. **1889.** Ward & Downey; first ed; cloth-backed pic. boards; 151 pp; Cr. 8vo [although the title page is dated 1889, the work was published in Dec. 1888]
548. **1895.** Ward & Downey; 7th ed; blue cloth, dec. & titled in red; Cr. 8vo

549. **1896.** Ward & Downey; 'Enterprise Library' Copyright Edition; dark-pink cloth, dec. in blind with floral design; titled gilt on spine; 151 pp; 15 pp. adverts at end; 8vo
550. **[n.d.** Copyright **1896].** Fenno, N.Y; first U.S. ed; light-blue cloth, front cover & spine dec. & titled white; 250 pp; 4 pp. cat. at end; Cr. 8vo
551. **1903.** Newnes; d.w. illus. by H. M. Brock
552. **[1909].** Newnes' Sixpenny Copyright Novels; 114 pp; pic. d.w; Sm 8vo
553. [*c.* **1912].** Hodder & Stoughton Sevenpenny Library; beige-brown cloth; dec. in blind, gilt; col. frontis; illus. 'Dramatis Personae'; 8vo

**The Mystery of Sasassa Valley**
554. **1879.** In: Chambers's Journal, Oct. issue [first published article of Conan Doyle's apart from schoolboy efforts — appeared anonymously]
555. **1886.** Story in: Dreamland and Ghostland, vol. III [q.v.]
556. **1899.** Story in: Peril & Prowse [q.v. item 1030]

MYSTERIES AND ADVENTURES
557. **[1889].** Walter Scott; first ed; buff paper wrappers, lettered on front cover and spine in black; 249 pp; 6 pp. adverts at end; 12 mo
558. **[1889].** Walter Scott; as above, variant binding in plum-red fine morocco-grain cloth; no imprint on spine; 12 mo (This book was re-issued in 1893 under the title of: *The Gully of Bluemansdyke and Other Stories* [q.v.])
559. **[n.d.].** Fenno, N.Y; green cloth, titled in red; Cr. 8vo

**My War Reading**
560. **1918.** In: The Book Monthly, Autumn issue [not in Locke]

**The Narrative of John Smith**
561. **1883.** An early novel; unpublished [not in Locke]

***The Naval Treaty [The Adventure of]**
562. **1893.** Story in: The Strand Magazine, Oct. issue; illus. by Sidney Paget
563. **1894.** Story in: The Memoirs of Sherlock Holmes [q.v.]

**The New Catacomb**
564. **1898.** Story in: Sunlight Year Book, under the title of: *Burger's Secret* [q.v.]
565. **1900.** Story in: The Green Flag [q.v.]

**A New Light on Old Crimes**
566. **1920.** In: The Strand Magazine

**The New Revelation or What is Spiritualism**
567. **1918.** Hodder & Stoughton; first ed; black cloth; gilt lettering on spine; 170 pp; Cr. 8vo
568. **[1918].** Doran, N.Y; first U.S. ed; green cloth, titled in red; Cr. 8vo
569. **1919.** Hodder & Stoughton, Toronto; 122 pp.
570. [*c.* **1924].** Hodder & Stoughton; 8th ed.

**A Night Among the Nihilists**
571. **[1889].** Story in: My Friend the Murderer [q.v.]
572. **[1889].** Story in: Mysteries and Adventures [q.v.]

**The Nightmare Room**
573. **1921.** In: The Strand Magazine

**The Night Patrol**
574. **1919.** Poem in: The Guards Came Through [q.v.]

**Night Voices**
575. **1911.** Poem in: Songs of the Road [q.v.]

**1902-1909**
576. **1911.** Poem in: Songs of the Road [q.v.]

***The Noble Bachelor [The Adventure of]**
577. **1892.** Story in: The Strand Magazine; Apr. issue; illus. by Sidney Paget
578. **1892.** Story in: The Adventures of Sherlock Holmes [q.v.]

***The Norwood Builder [The Adventure of]**
579. **1903.** Story in: The Strand Magazine, Nov. issue; illus. by Sidney Paget
580. **1903.** Story in: The Return of Sherlock Holmes [q.v.]

**Now then Smith**
581. **1922.** Poem in: The Strand Magazine, Jul. issue
582. **1922.** In: The Poems of Arthur Conan Doyle [q.v.]

**The Old Gray Fox**
583. **1898.** Poem in: Songs of Action [q.v.]

**The Old Huntsman**
584. **1898.** Poem in: Songs of Action [q.v.]

**An Old Story Retold**
585. **1920.** In: The Strand Magazine

**On Books**
586. **1894.** In: Great Thoughts, May & Jun. issues [not in Locke]

**One Crowded Hour**
587. **1911.** Story in: The Strand Magazine; illus. by H. M. Brock
588. **1918.** In: Danger! And Other Stories [q.v.]

**On the Intemperance of Our Country**
589. **[1870's].** First published work of Arthur Conan Doyle's; apparently written by him in his early teens when a school boy at Stonyhurst; probably appeared in one of the school's magazines [not in Locke]

**An Open Letter to Those of My Generation**
590. **[1929].** Psychic Press; wrappers; 12 pp. [not in Locke]

**The Orphange**
591. **1911.** Poem in: Songs of the Road [q.v.]

OUR AFRICAN WINTER
592. **1929.** Murray; first ed; frontis; 289 pp.
593. **1929.** Hodder & Stoughton

OUR AMERICAN ADVENTURE
594. **[1923].** Hodder & Stoughton; first ed; frontis; blue cloth, gilt lettered; 205 pp; Demy 8vo
595. **[1923].** Doran, N.Y; first U.S. ed; frontis; cloth titled in green; d.w. (Second vol. of a trilogy with The Wanderings of a Spiritualist [q.v.] and Our Second American Adventure [q.v.])

**Our Derby Sweepstakes**
596. **1881.** Unpublished

**Our Midnight Visitor**
597. 1891. Temple Bar, Feb. issue [not in Locke]

**Our Reply to the Cleric Press**
598. 1920. Spiritualist Union; wrappers

OUR SECOND AMERICAN ADVENTURE
599. **[1924].** Hodder & Stoughton; first ed; illus; blue fine-ribbed cloth, gilt; 250 pp; Demy 8vo
600. **1924.** Little, Brown, Boston; first U.S. ed; illus; green cloth, gilt; Demy 8vo
(The third vol. of a trilogy with The Wanderings of a Spiritualist [q.v.] and Our American Adventure [q.v.])

**The Outcasts**
601. **1911.** Poem in: Songs of the Road [q.v.]

**An Outing in Wartime**
602. **1915.** In: The Strand Magazine

**Out of the Running**
603. **1911.** Story in: The Last Galley [q.v.]

**A Parable**
604. **1898.** Poem in: Songs of Action [q.v.]
605. **1919.** Poem in: The Guards Came Through [q.v.]

THE PARASITE. A NOVEL
606. **1894.** Archibald Constable — The Acme Library series; first ed; pale green wrappers, titled in dark-green; 125 pp. [scarce]
607. **1894.** As above, variant binding in blue fine-ribbed cloth, pic. blocked & titled in gilt; t.e.g; 125 pp; 2 pp. adverts at end; Sm 8vo (reprinted Dec. 1894 and Jan. 1895) [not in Locke]
608. **1897.** Archibald Constable; yellow cloth, pic. blocked & titled in black & red; 125 pp; Slim 8vo (reprinted 1898)
609. **1897.** As above, variant binding blocked in black only [very scarce]

THE PARASITE. A STORY
610. **1895.** Harper & Bros.; N.Y; first U.S. ed; illus. by Howard Pyle; grey cloth, titled & dec. gilt; Cr. 8vo

**The Parish Magazine**
611. **1930.** Story in: The Strand Magazine

**The Parson of Jackman's Gulch**
612. **1885.** Story in: London Society, Extra Christmas Number [not in Locke]
613. **1889.** In: My Friend The Murderer and Other Tales of Mystery and Adventure [q.v.]
614. **1889.** In: Mysteries and Adventures [q.v.]
615. **1890.** In: The Captain of the Pole-Star and Other Tales [q.v.]

**The Passage of the Red Sea**
616. **1873.** A poem [not in Lcoke]

**The Passing of the Legions**
617. **[1911?].** A sketch [Nordon, p. 317 — not in Locke]

**Pennarby Mine**
618. **1893.** Poem in: The Pall Mall Magazine, Aug. issue; illus.
619. **1898.** Poem in: Songs of Action [q.v.]

**A Petition to the Prime Minister**
620. **[1916?].** Privately printed [not in Locke]

PHENEAS SPEAKS. **Direct Spirit Communications in the Family Circle Reported by Sir Arthur Conan Doyle**
621. **[1927].** The Psychic Press & Simpkin Marshall; first ed; frontis; pale-blue cloth, spine titled white; 216 pp; 4 pp. adverts at end; Cr. 8vo

**A Physiologist's Wife**
622. [*c.* **1885].** A tragi-comedy. Unpublished

**Pirates and Blue Water [Tales of]**
623. **[1921].** Murray Uniform Edition; first ed; pale-blue paper boards, pic. blocked in blind, gilt; contains stories published for the first time; 308 pp; 8vo
624. **1929.** In: The Conan Doyle Stories Omnibus [q.v.]

**Playing with Fire**
625. **1900.** Story in: The Strand Magazine
626. **1908.** In: Round The Fire Stories [q.v.]

THE POEMS OF ARTHUR CONAN DOYLE. **Collected Edition**
627. **1922.** Murray; first ed; Preface dated March 1922; blue cloth, gilt lettered on spine; 242 pp; Cr. 8vo
628. **1928.** Murray; Cheaper Edition; new Preface dated June 1928; light-blue boards, front cover and spine dec. & titled in blind & gilt; 242 pp; 2 pp. adverts at end; Sm. 8vo

**[Collected] Poems of Sir Arthur Conan Doyle**
629. **1939.** Murray; Cheaper Edition; light-blue cloth; author's facsimile signature in darker blue on front cover; spine titled in darker blue; pic. d.w; Sm. 8vo

**A Point of Contact**
630. **1922.** In: The Story-Teller, Oct. issue

**A Point of View**
631. **1918.** In: Danger! And Other Stories [q.v.]
632. **[1922].** Story in: Tales of Long Ago [q.v.]

THE POISON BELT. **[Being an Account of Another Adventure of Prof. E. Challenger, Lord John Roxton, Prof. Summerlee: & Mr. E. D. Malone, the Discoverers of 'The Lost World']**
633. **1913.** In: The Strand Magazine; illus. by Harry Rountree (serialised)
634. **1913.** Hodder & Stoughton; first ed; 16 illus. by Harry Rountree; blue cloth, pic. blocked & titled in black on front cover; pic. spine in black and gilt; 199 pp; Cr. 8vo
635. **1913.** Hodder & Stoughton & Doran, N.Y; first U.S. ed; 16 illus. by Harry Rountree; red fine-grain cloth, front cover & spine titled in gilt extra; 252 pp; Cr. 8vo
636. **[n.d.]** Hodder & Stoughton; red boards, black titling on spine; 199 pp; Sm. 8vo
637. **1952.** In: The Professor Challenger Stories Omnibus [q.v.]

**A Post-Impressionist**
638. **1911.** Poem in: Songs of the Road [q.v.]

**The Pot of Caviare**
639. **1908.** Story in: The Strand Magazine; illus. by R. Caton Woodville
640. **1908.** In: Round The Fire Stories [q.v.]
641. **1912.** Adaptation of the story as a play; performed but unpublished

***The Priory School [The Adventure of]**
642. **1904.** Story in: The Strand Magazine, Feb. issue; Illus. by Sidney Paget
643. **1905.** Story in: The Return of Sherlock Holmes [q.v.]

**The Prisoner's Defence**
644. **1916.** Story in: The Strand Magazine
645. **1918.** Story in: Danger! And Other Stories [q.v.]
646. **1959.** Story in: Ellery Queen's Mystery Magazine, Nov. issue

***The Problem of Thor Bridge**
*see* **Thor Bridge** [q.v.]

**Psychic Experiences**
647. **1925.** Putnam; wrappers (reprinted from a work entitled: 'Survival')

**A Question of Diplomacy**
648. **1894.** Story in: Round The Red Lamp [q.v.]
649. **1895.** Adaptation of the story as a one-act play, performed, but unpublished

**A Race Against Time**
650. **1928.** Pitman; in Pitman's shorthand

**Ragtime!**
651. **1919.** Poem in: The Guards Came Through [q.v.]

**The Recollections of Captain Wilkie**
652. **1895.** In: Chambers's Journal, Jan. issue [not in Locke]

***The Red Circle [The Adventure of]**
653. **1911.** Story in: The Strand Magazine, Mar. & Apr. issues; illus. by H. M. Brock and Joseph Simpson
654. Story in: His Last Bow [q.v.]

***The Red-Headed League [The Adventure of]**
655. **1891.** Story in: The Strand Magazine, Aug. issue; illus. by Sidney Paget
656. **1892.** Story in: The Adventures of Sherlock Holmes [q.v.]
657. **1962.** Story in: Ellery Queen's Mystery Magazine, Jan. issue

**The Red Star**
658. **1911.** Story in: The Last Galley [q.v.]
659. **[1922].** Story in: Tales of Long Ago [q.v.]

THE REFUGEES. **A Tale of Two Continents**
660. **1893.** In: Harper's Magazine (serialised)
661. **1893.** Longmans, Green; first ed; green cloth, ruled borders in blind; spines dec. & titled in dark-green; 3 vols: vol. I, 227 pp; 24 pp. cat. dated '3.93' at end; vol. II, 214 pp; vol. III, 304 pp; Cr. 8vo
662. **1893.** Longmans, Green; New and Cheaper Edition; one-vol; (reprinted twice 1893; once 1894; twice 1895)
663. **1893.** Longmans, Green; Colonial one-vol. ed. (reprinted twice 1893; once 1895; once 1896 and once 1898)
664. **[1893].** Harper & Bros; N.Y; first U.S. ed; illus. by T. De Thulstrup; blue diagonal fine-grain cloth, dec. gilt & titled red; Cr. 8vo
665. **[*c.* 1893].** Tauchnitz Copyright Edition; Leipzig; 2 vols; Sm. 8vo
666. **1894.** Longmans, Green; New Edition; grey-green cloth over bevelled boards, titled gilt on front cover & spine; 384 pp; Cr. 8vo
667. **1895.** Longmans, Green; New Edition; first English illus. ed; 25 illus. by T. De Thulstrup; plum-red cloth, dec. & titled silver; 384 pp; 32 pp. cat. at end; Cr. 8vo (reprinted 1896, 1898, 1901 and 1903)
668. **1903.** Longmans, Green; New Edition; plum-red buckram, ruled border in gilt on front cover; dec. & titled spine; gilt; 384 pp; no cat. at end; Cr. 8vo (items 667-8 in the Silver Library Edition)
669. **[n.d.]** Nelson's Copyright Novels; frontis; Sm. 8vo
670. **1931.** In: The Conan Doyle Historical Romances Omnibus [q.v.]
671. **1949.** Murray Uniform Edition; 384 pp; pic. d.w; Cr. 8vo

**A Regency Tale**
672. **1930.** This is Conan Doyle's last story; unpublished [*see* Dickson Carr, p. 337]

**A Regimental Scandal**
673. **1892.** This story appeared in two American newspapers in May 1892 and has never been published in bookform [originally entitled: *The Mayor's Card*]

***The Reigate Squires [The Adventure of]**
674. **1893.** Story in: The Strand Magazine, Jun. issue; illus. by Sidney Paget
675. **1894.** Story in: The Memoirs of Sherlock Holmes [q.v.]

**Religio Medici**
676. **1911.** Poem in: Songs of the Road [q.v.]

677. **The Religion of the Future**
*see* **If I Were a Preacher** [q.v. item 1021]

**A Reminiscence of Cricket**
678. **1922.** In: The Poems of Arthur Conan Doyle [q.v.]

**Reply to Col. Lonsdale Hale on Home Defence**
679. **1901.** In: The Nineteenth Century, Mar. issue

***The Resident Patient [The Adventure of]**
680. **1893.** Story in: The Strand Magazine, Aug. issue; illus. by Sidney Paget
681. **1894.** Story in: The Memoirs of Sherlock Holmes [q.v.]

***The Resident Patient and Other Stories from The Adventures and Memoirs**
682. **[1921].** Newnes' Sevenpenny Novels; 128 pp; Sm. 8vo

***The Retired Colourman [The Adventure of]**
683. **1927.** Story in: The Strand Magazine, Jan. issue; illus. by Frank Wiles
684. **1927.** Story in: The Case-Book of Sherlock Holmes [q.v.]

**The Retirement of Signor Lambert**
685. **1898.** In: Cosmopolitan, Dec. issue [not in Locke]

**Retrospect**
686. **1922.** In: The Poems of Arthur Conan Doyle [q.v.]

*THE RETURN OF SHERLOCK HOLMES
687. **1903-4.** In: The Strand Magazine; illus. by Sidney Paget (serialised)
688. **1905.** Newnes; first ed; 16 illus. by Sidney Paget; blue cloth, front cover & spine titled gilt; 403 pp; 4 pp. adverts at end; Cr. 8vo
689. **1905.** McClure, Phillips, N.Y; first U.S. ed; illus. by Charles Raymond Macauley; 381 pp; 8vo
690. **[1905].** Collier, N.Y; in 'The Latest Books of Conan Doyle' series; cloth dec. with the author's initials within a floral panel in blind, with his full name gilt; Demy 8vo
691. **[1905].** Morang; Toronto; 381 pp. 8vo
692. **1907.** A. Wessels, N.Y; illus. by Charles Raymond Macauley; pic. cloth; 8vo
693. **1908.** Newnes; same as first ed; bound in red cloth, *not* blue
694. **[1913].** Newnes' Sixpenny Copyright Novels; 156 pp; Sm. 8vo
695. **1915.** Smith, Elder; New Edition; 16 illus. by Sidney Paget; red cloth, gilt; 403 pp; 4 pp. adverts at end; Cr. 8vo
696. **[1915-19].** Pitman; Engraved in the Advanced Stage of Pitman's Shorthand. By Permission of the Author; New Era Edition; illus. by Sidney Paget (vol. 2 & 3 only); blue cloth; ruled borders & title etc. in black; 8vo; 3 vols: vol. 1, 120 pp; 12 pp. adverts at end; vol. II, 130 pp; 6 pp. adverts at end; vol. III, 120 pp; 8 pp. adverts at end
697. **1924.** Murray; Thin Paper Edition: red fine-grain cloth; author's intials on front cover in gilt; spine dec. & titled gilt; 248 pp; Sm. 8vo

**The Ring and the Camp [Tales of]**
698. **[1922].** Murray 'Uniform Edition'; first ed; blue paper boards, blocked pic. in blind, gilt; contains some stories published for the first time; 8vo
699. **1929.** In: The Conan Doyle Stories Omnibus [q.v.]

**The Ring of Toth**
700. **1890.** Story in: The Strand Magazine, Jan. issue
701. **1890.** Story in: The Captain of the Pole-Star and Other Stories [q.v.]
702. [*c.* **1892**]. In: The Sign of the Four. A Scandal in Bohemia — And Other Stories [q.v.]

RODNEY STONE
703. **1896.** In: The Strand Magazine; illus. by Sidney Paget (serialised)
704. **1896.** Smith, Elder; first ed; 8 illus. by Sidney Paget; dark-blue diced-grain cloth, dec. with an anchor & titled gilt on front cover & spine; 366 pp; 10 pp. adverts at end; Cr. 8vo
705. **1896.** Smith, Elder; first ed; sp. bound for Mudie's Library; contents same as first ed; pink cloth over bevelled boards, blocked with floral design in gilt on front cover & spine; spine lettered gilt; Mudie's stamp in blind on back cover; Cr. 8vo (no adverts at end)
706. **1896.** Bell's Indian & Colonial Library Edition; first ed. thus; 8 illus. by Sidney Paget; light-pink cloth, lettered in brown on front cover & spine; 366 pp; Bohn's Library cat. at end; Cr. 8vo
707. **1896.** Appleton, N.Y; first U.S. ed; 12 illus. by Sidney Paget; brown-red buckram, dec. & titled silver & gilt on front cover & spine; 408 pp; 14 pp. adverts at end; Cr. 8vo (reprinted 1897)

708. **[1901].** In a Prize Volume, consisting of three Newnes' Sixpenny Novels; "Rodney Stone", illus. by Sidney Paget; George R. Sims' "Memoirs of a Mother-in-law", illus. by H. M. Brock, and Mrs. Humphrey Ward's "Marcella"; red fine-ribbed cloth over bevelled boards, florally blocked in black, titled gilt; a.e.g; Demy 8vo (not in Locke]
709. **1901.** Newnes' Sixpenny Library; 122 pp; Sm. 8vo
710. **1906.** Smith, Elder; Third Edition; 8 illus. by Sidney Paget; red fine-grain cloth; front cover & spine blocked & titled in gilt; 366 pp; 10 pp. adverts at end; Cr. 8vo
711. [*c.* **1907**]. Smith, Elder; New and Cheaper Edition; 8 illus. by Sidney Paget; Cr. 8vo
712. **[1919].** Newnes' Sixpenny Copyright Novels; 122 pp; Sm. 8vo
713. [*c.* **1920**]. Nelson; pink boards; Cr. 8vo
714. **1930.** Murray; Cheaper Edition; bright-blue cloth; front cover dec. in blind; spine dec. & titled gilt; 378 pp; pic. d.w; Sm. 8vo (reprinted 1932)
715. **1932.** In: The Conan Doyle Historical Romances [q.v.]

THE ROMAN CATHOLIC CHURCH. A **Rejoinder**
716. **1929.** Psychic Press; buff wrappers, lettered black; adverts on inside of back cover; 72 pp; Sm. 8vo

ROUND THE FIRE STORIES
717. **1898.** In: The Strand Magazine; illus. by A. G. Hartrick, Frank Craig, Sidney Paget, etc. (serialised)
718. **1908.** Smith, Elder; first ed; frontis. by A. Castaigne; red cloth, front cover pic. blocked & titled gilt; gilt lettering on spine; 372 pp; 4 pp. cat. at end; Cr. 8vo
719. **1908.** McClure Co; N.Y; first U.S. ed; 8vo
720. **1922.** Murray; 'Uniform Edition'; 8vo

ROUND THE RED LAMP. **Being Facts and Fancies of Medical Life**
721. **1894.** Methuen; first ed; red fine-ribbed cloth, gilt; 328 pp; 32 pp. adverts at end, dated October 1894; Cr. 8vo
722. **1894.** Methuen; Second Edition; identical to first ed.
723. **1894.** Appleton, N.Y; first U.S. ed; red buckram, dec. & titled gilt & silver; 307 pp; 4 pp. adverts at end; Cr. 8vo
724. **1901.** Methuen; 7th ed; Cr. 8vo
725. **[1920].** Newnes' Copyright Novels No. 268; 124 pp; Sm. 8vo
726. **1934.** Murray; 'Uniform Edition'; red cloth, facsimile signature of the author on front cover in black; spine lettered black; pic. d.w; Cr. 8vo

**A Rover Chanty**
727. **1898.** Poem in: Songs of Action [q.v.]

***A Scandal in Bohemia**
728. **1891.** Story in: The Strand Magazine, Jul. issue; illus. by Sidney Paget
729. **1892.** Story in: The Adventures of Sherlock Holmes [q.v.]
730. [*c.* **1892**]. In: The Sign of the Four. A Scandal in Bohemia — And Other Stories [q.v.]
731. [*c.* **1895**]. Optimus Printing Co; N.Y; 'Handy Classics' series of 'Choice Stories by Famous Authors' No. 13; wrappers; 32 pp. [very scarce]

**The Sealed Room [The Story of]**
732. **1898.** Story in: The Strand Magazine; illus. by Claude A. Shepperson
733. **1908.** In: Round The Fire Stories [q.v.]

***The Second Stain [The Adventure of]**
734. **1904.** Story in: The Strand Magazine, Dec. issue; illus. by Sidney Paget
735. **1905.** Story in: The Return of Sherlock Holmes [q.v.]

**Sexagenarius Loquitur**
736. **1911.** Poem in: Songs of the Road [q.v.]

**A Shadow Before**
737. **1900.** Story in: The Green Flag [q.v.]

**The Shadow on the Screen**
738. **1920.** In: The Strand Magazine

**Shakespeare's Expostulation**
739. **1909.** Poem in: The Cornhill Magazine, Mar. issue
740. **1911.** Poem in: Songs of the Road [q.v.]

***Sherlock Holmes — A Play. By Arthur Conan Doyle [sic] and William Gillette**
741. **[1922].** Samuel French, London and N.Y; wrappers
742. **1935.** Doubleday, N.Y; portrait frontis; 191 pp; wrappers
*see also* **William Gillette, Sherlock Holmes, A Play** [q.v. item 1102]

***Shoscombe Old Place [The Adventure of]**
743. **1927.** Story in: The Strand Magazine, Apr. issue; illus. by Frank Wiles
744. **1927.** Story in: The Case-Book of Sherlock Holmes [q.v.]

**The Siege of Sunda Gunge**
745. [*c.* **1895**]. Optimus Printing Co; N.Y; 'Handy Classics' series of 'Choice Stories by Famous Authors'; wrappers; 30 pp. [Doyle has denied the authorship of this story — not in Locke]

*THE SIGN OF [THE] FOUR
746. **1890.** In: Lippincott's Magazine; Feb. issue; one illus.
747. **1890.** In: Six Complete Stories from Lippincott [q.v. item 1037]

748. **1890.** Spencer Blackett; first ed; frontis. by Charles Kerr; red-brown cloth, dec. borders in black, titled gilt; 283 pp; 32 pp. adverts at end; Cr. 8vo
749. **1890.** Spencer Blackett; first ed; variant, with the imprint of Griffith, Farran & Co. on spine; no adverts at end
750. **[1891].** Tauchnitz Copyright Edition, Leipzig; Sm. 8vo
751. **1892.** Newnes; first ed; second issue; not to be confused with the Second Edition [see below]; same as first ed. in every respect, but with a different title-page [Locke, p. 30]
752. **1892.** Newnes; Second Edition; no frontis; brown diagonal fine-ribbed cloth, pic. blocked & titled in black & colours on front and spine; flowered e.p.s.; 283 pp; Cr. 8vo
753. **1892.** As above; variant binding in *red* cloth, pic. blocked & titled in black & colours on front cover and spine
754. **1893.** Newnes; Third Edition; red diagonal fine-ribbed cloth, pic. blocked & titled in black & bright colours; Cr. 8vo
755. **1893.** Newnes; as above; variant binding in maroon, horizontal fine-ribbed cloth, pic. blocked in black, grey, white, primrose and orange; Cr. 8vo
756. **1894.** Newnes; New Edition; bright-blue cloth, blocked with 'Strand Library' motif & titling in black & gilt; 283 pp; Cr. 8vo
757. **[1896?].** Newnes; 25th Thou.
758. **[1898].** Pitman; in Pitman's Shorthand; gray cloth, dec. & titled in red & gilt; 171 pp; 8vo (reprinted 1905)
759. **[1903].** Newnes; Souvenir Edition; first illus. ed; 8 illus. by F. H. Townsend; blue cloth, pic. blocked & titled gilt; publisher's device in blind on back cover; t.e.g; 285 pp; Cr. 8vo
760. **[1908].** Smith, Elder; New Edition; 8 illus. by F. H. Townsend; red cloth, titled gilt; 285 pp; 10 pp. adverts at end; Cr. 8vo
761. **[1916].** Pitman; in Pitman's Shorthand; 'Centenary Edition'; green cloth, double-ruled borders & titled in blind; spine titled in gilt; 171 pp; Sm. 8vo
762. **[1918].** The Gregg Pub. Co; N.Y; Printed in Gregg Shorthand; buff cloth, front cover dec. & titled black; no titling on spine; 188 pp; 8vo
763. **[1926].** Pitman, London & N.Y; Printed in the Advanced Style of Pitman's Shorthand; New Era Edition; light-blue linen-weave cloth, ruled border & publisher's device in blind; titled gilt; 170 pp; 14 pp. adverts at end; Sm. 8vo (reprinted 1942)
764. **[n.d.].** Newnes; Cheap Edition; 124 pp; Cr. 8vo
765. **[n.d.].** Newnes; 'The Penny Library of Famous Books', No. 9; wrappers printed in green; 8vo
766. **[n.d.].** Newnes; The Sixpenny Series of Copyright Books; red wrappers, pic. titled in black; 124 pp; 4 pp. adverts; Demy 8vo
767. **[n.d.].** Nelson's Copyright Novels; frontis; Sm. 8vo
768. **1949.** Royle; light-green cloth, titled in dark-green; pic. d.w. with Abbey's portrait of Sherlock Holmes; Cr. 8vo
769. **[n.d.].** The Mershon Co; N.Y; maroon cloth, front & back cover dec. in blind; gilt lettering on spine; 189 pp; Cr. 8vo
770. **[The Sign of the Four.] The Surgeon of Gaster Fell [And Other Stories]**
*see* **The Surgeon of Gaster Fell** [q.v.]

**The Sign of the Four. A Scandal in Bohemia — And Other Stories** (also contains: A Case of Identity; My Friend the Murderer; The Ring of Toth; The Surgeon of Gaster Fell & John Huxford's Hiatus)
771. [*c.* **1892**]. A. L. Burt Co; N.Y; first U.S. ed; dark-red diagonal fine-ribbed cloth, spine dec. & titled gilt; 364 pp; Cr. 8vo [scarce]
[For detailed information consult: Nathan (L. Bengis), **The 'Signs' of Our Times. An Irregular Bibliography,** N.Y; 1956 — A Bibliography of The Sign of Four]

***Silver Blaze [The Adventure of]**
772. **1892.** Story in: The Strand Magazine, Dec. issue; illus. by Sidney Paget
773. **1894.** Story in: The Memoirs of Sherlock Holmes [q.v.]
774. **1931.** Story in: The Detective in Fiction [q.v. item 1010]

**The Silver Hatchet**
775. **1883.** Story in: London Society, Christmas Number
776. [*c.* **1890**]. Story in: My Friend the Murderer and Other Mysteries and Adventures [q.v.]
777. **[1889].** Story in: Mysteries and Adventures [q.v.]

**The Silver Mirror**
778. **1908.** Story in: The Strand Magazine, Aug. issue; illus. by Arthur Twidle
779. **1911.** Story in: The Last Galley [q.v.]
780. **[1920].** Story in: Tales of Long Ago [q.v.]

**The Singular Experiences of Mr. John Scott Eccles**
781. **1908.** In: The Strand Magazine; illus. by Arthur Twidle

SIR NIGEL
782. **1905-6.** In: The Strand Magazine; illus. by Arthur Twidle (serialised)
783. **1906.** Smith, Elder; first ed; 8 illus. by Arthur Twidle; red cloth, pic. blocked & titled gilt; 394 pp; 2 pp. adverts at end; Cr. 8vo

784. **1906.** McClure, Phillips; first U.S. ed; illus. by The Kinneys; pale blue ribbed cloth, pic. blocked & titled in black & dark-green; Cr. 8vo
785. **1906.** William Briggs, Toronto; first Canadian ed; 346 pp; 8vo
786. **1912.** Smith, Elder; New Edition; same binding as first ed. but rougher cloth and not pic. blocked; Cr. 8vo
787. **1924.** Murray; first Thin Paper Edition; red fine-grain cloth; author's initials on front cover, gilt; 248 pp; Sm. 8vo
788. **1931.** In: The Conan Doyle Historical Romances Omnibus [q.v.]
789. **[n.d.].** Nelson's Copyright Novels; frontis; Sm. 8vo
790. **1976.** Murray; introduced by Mary Renault; first ed. thus; d.w; 8vo

**Sir Nigel's Song**
791. **1911.** Poem in: Songs of the Road [q.v.]

***The Six Napoleons [The Adventure of]**
792. **1904.** Story in: The Strand Magazine, May issue; illus. by Sidney Paget
793. **1905.** Story in: The Return of Sherlock Holmes [q.v.]

**The "Slapping Sal"**
794. **1900.** Story in: The Green Flag [q.v.]
795. **[n.d.].** Story in: The Great Shadow and Other Napoleonic Tales [q.v.]

**A Soldier's Prayer**
*see* **The Souvenir of the Charing Cross Hospital Bazaar** [q.v. item 1038]

***The Solitary Cyclist [The Adventure of]**
796. **1904.** Story in: The Strand Magazine, Jan. issue; illus. by Sidney Paget
797. **1905.** Story in: The Return of Sherlock Holmes [q.v.]

**Some Military Lessons of the War**
798. **1900.** In: The Cornhill Magazine, Oct. issue
799. **1900.** Last chapter of: The Great Boer War [q.v.]

***Some Personalia about Mr. Sherlock Holmes**
800. **1917.** In: The Strand Magazine

**Some Recollections of Sport**
801. **1909.** In: The Strand Magazine; illus. by Arthur Twidle

**The Song of the Bow**
802. **1898.** Poem in: Songs of Action [q.v.]

SONGS OF ACTION
803. **1898.** Smith, Elder; first ed; blue buckram, dec. & titled gilt on front cover; spine titled gilt; 136 pp; Sm. Cr. 8vo
804. **1898.** Doubleday, N.Y; first U.S. ed; red buckram, gilt; t.e.g; Slim 8vo
805. **1909.** Smith Elder; 6th impr; Cr. 8vo [identical to first ed.] (reprinted 1916)
806. **[1919].** Murray; 7th impr.
(Most of the poems contained in this volume appear later in: The Poems of Arthur Conan Doyle [q.v.])

SONGS OF THE ROAD
807. **1911.** Smith Elder; first ed; blue buckram pic. blocked and titled gilt, front cover; spine titled gilt; 137 pp; Sm. Cr. 8vo
808. **1919.** Murray
(Most of the poems contained in this volume appear later in: The Poems of Arthur Conan Doyle [q.v.])

***The Speckled Band [The Adventure of]**
809. **1892.** Story in: The Strand Magazine, Feb. issue; illus. by Sidney Paget
810. **1892.** Story in: The Adventures of Sherlock Holmes [q.v.]
811. **1934.** Story in: A Century of Thrillers From Poe to Arlen [q.v. item 1006]
812. **[1937].** Story in: Century of Thrillers [q.v. item 1007]

***The Speckled Band — An Adventure of Sherlock Holmes [A Play]**
813. **1912.** Samuel French, N.Y; 124 pp; 8vo
814. **[1912].** As above; second issue, with publisher's address changed to: 25 West 45th Street, N.Y.

**Spiritualism and Rationalism**
815. **[1920].** Hodder & Stoughton; wrappers; 32 pp.
816. [*c.* **1924**]. Hodder & Stoughton; third thou.

**The Spiritualist's Reader . . . Compiled by Sir Arthur Conan Doyle**
817. **1924.** Two Worlds Publishing Co; Manchester; first ed; frontis; green morocco-grain cloth, dec. in blind; titled on front cover only, in white; 158 pp; Cr. 8vo
818. **1924.** As above; variant binding in blue cloth; white lettering on front cover and spine

THE STARK MUNRO LETTERS
819. **1894-5.** In: The Idler Magazine; illus. by George Hutchinson (serialised)
820. **1895.** Longmans, Green; first ed; frontis. & vignette title page; blue cloth over bevelled boards; gilt lettering on front cover & spine; 346 pp; 24 pp. adverts at end, dated July 1895; Cr. 8vo
821. **1895.** Tauchnitz Copyright Edition, Leipzig; 8vo
822. **[1908].** Amalgamated Press; Daily Mail Sixpenny Series; 3 illus. by Edmund J. Sullivan; paper wrappers; 162 pp; 8vo
823. **[n.d.].** Newnes' Sixpenny Copyright Novels; Sm. 8vo

***The Stockbroker's Clerk [The Adventure of]**
824. **1893.** Story in: The Strand Magazine, Mar. issue; illus. by Sidney Paget

825. **1894.** Story in: The Memoirs of Sherlock Holmes [q.v.]

**The Stone of Boxman's Drift**
826. **1887.** In: Boy's Own Annual

**The Storming Party**
827. **1898.** Poem in: Songs of Action [q.v.]

**The Story of B.24**
828. **1899.** Story in: The Strand Magazine; illus. by Sidney Paget
829. **1908.** Story in: Round The Fire Stories [q.v.]

**The Story of Mr. George Edalji**
830. **1907.** H.M. Stationery Office; wrappers; 17 pp; 8vo [not in Locke]
*see also* **The Case of Mr. George Edalji** [q.v.]

**[The Story of] Waterloo — A Play in One Act**
831. **[1907].** Samuel French; first ed; mauve wrappers, pic. blocked & titled, etc. in black; cover design by G. Thorp; 19 pp; 8vo
*see also* **One-Act Plays of Today** [q.v. item 1029] (Dramatization of a short story entitled: *A Straggler of* '15 in: Round The Red Lamp [q.v.])

**A Straggler of '15**
832. **1894.** Story in: Round The Red Lamp [q.v.]
*see also* **[The Story of] Waterloo** (above)

**The Strange Case of George Edalji**
*see* **The Case of George Edalji**
*see also* **Famous Crimes, Mysteries & Romances** [q.v. item 1013]

**Strange Secrets**
833. [*c.* **1896**]. Fenno, N.Y; blue cloth, dec. & titled in white on front cover & spine; 8vo (listed in publisher's cat. at end of 'The Mystery of Cloomber' [q.v.] as: "Uniform with this Volume")

**Strange Studies from Life**
834. **1901.** In: The Strand Magazine, Mar; Apr. and May issues (Three Studies in the History of Crime: The Holocaust of Manor Place; The Love Affair of George Vincent Parker, and The Debatable Case of Mrs. Emsley)

**Stranger Than Fiction**
835. **1915.** In: The Strand Magazine, Dec. issue; illus. by Thomas Somerfield

**The Striped Chest**
836. **1900.** Story in: The Green Flag [q.v.]

*A STUDY IN SCARLET **[The Reminiscences of John H. Watson. M.D.]**
837. **[1887?].** Mentioned in Beeton's Christmas Annual, but according to The World Bibliography [p. 19, No. 415]: "A book so scarce that it has yet to be located."
[It would appear that Ward, Lock intended to publish it in 1887, advertised it in *Beeton's Christmas Annual*, and then had a change of heart; *see* Higham, [p. 75]: "Ward Lock . . . accepted it [in 1887], bought all the rights for twenty-four pounds, and said the story would appear about a year later" . . . which it did]
838. **1887.** In: Beeton's Christmas Annual; 3 illus. by D. H. Friston; 1 illus. by W. M. R. Quick; 138 pp; pic. wrappers; $8\frac{1}{4}$ x $5\frac{1}{2}$ in. [very scarce]
839. **1888.** Ward, Lock; first ed. in book form; 6 illus. by Charles Doyle (the author's father); paper wrappers; 169 pp; 2 pp. adverts at end; Cr. 8vo (Reprinted same year; according to Locke, reprinted in 1889)
840. **1890.** Lippincott, Philadelphia; first U.S. ed; Lippincott Series of Select Novels, No. 107; wrappers; 214 pp; 2 pp. adverts at end; Sm 8vo
841. **1891.** Ward, Lock; New Edition; first fully illus. ed; 40 illus. by Geo Hutchinson; buff cloth; front cover titled in red; spine titled in gilt; green flowered e.p.s; 224 pp; 24 pp. adverts at end; Cr. 8vo (reprinted 1893)
842. [*c.* **1892**]. Ward, Lock; frontis; red cloth, pic. blocked with a portrait of Sherlock Holmes & titling within a box, in black; 8vo (reprinted same year)
843. **[1893].** Ward, Lock; with a Note on Sherlock Holmes by Dr. Joseph Bell (reprinted from *The Bookman* [q.v. item 1090]; 40 illus. by Geo. Hutchinson; first ed. thus with the 'Note' reprinted from *The Bookman*; buff cloth, titled in red; red cloth spine; Cr. 8vo (reprinted several times)
844. [*c.* **1893**]. Tauchnitz Copyright Edition, Leipzig; Sm. 8vo [not in Locke]
845. [*c.* **1893**]. A Study In Scarlet. A Detective Story. A New Edition; Lever Brothers, Port Sunlight; 40 illus. by Geo Hutchinson; pic. glazed 'yellow-back' type boards; Cr. 8vo
846. **[1895]. A Study In Scarlet. A Novel;** Strawbridge & Clothier, Philadelphia; pic. wrappers, depicting a portrait of a girl in a large hat; 8vo [pirated?]
847. **[1895]**. Optimus Printing Co; N.Y; buff cloth florally dec. & titled in maroon-brown; 8vo
848. **A Study In Scarlet. [Being a Reprint from the Reminiscences of John H. Watson. M.D., late of Army Medical Department]**
**1895.** Ward, Lock & Bowden; issued as a supplement to the **Windsor Magazine Christmas Number;** illus. by James Greig; pic. wrappers [see cover illus. of this Bibliography]; 64 pp. [very scarce]
849. **[1901].** Ward, Lock; with a Note on Sherlock Holmes by Dr. Joseph Bell [q.v. item 1090]; reprint; 40 illus. by Geo. Hutchinson; green fine-ribbed cloth, dec. with panels, etc. in blind; titled within a frame; gilt; Cr. 8vo
850. **1904. A Study in Scarlet and The Sign of Four;** Harper & Bros; N.Y; light-blue cloth, dec. in black, titled gilt; Cr. 8vo

851. **1911. A Study In Scarlet. The First Book About Sherlock Holmes;** Ward Lock; reprint; frontis. & text illus. by Geo Hutchinson; 2 illus. by James Greig, one (unsigned) on art paper; red cloth, dec. with motif of sunshine streaming through the windows, in blind; titled gilt; 224 pp; 16 pp. adverts at end; Cr. 8vo
852. [*c.* **1920].** Ward, Lock; red cloth, front cover pic. blocked with portrait of Sherlock Holmes in black & titled black; spine titled black; 255 pp; 1 p. advertisement for The Windsor Magazine at end (The volume includes a Publisher's Note, and an introductory note entitled: "Mr. Sherlock Holmes" by Dr. Joseph Bell — not in World Bibliography)
853. **[n.d.].** Ward, Lock; contents as item 849; Cheap Edition, with 'Publisher's Note to This Edition'; printed in double-column; cloth; Cr. 8vo
854. **[n.d.].** Lever Brothers, Port Sunlight; contents as item 845; Sixpenny Edition; col. pic. glazed wrappers; 96 pp; Demy 8vo (adverts on back cover for Sunlight Soap, and a col. illus. by Hassall)
856. **[n.d.]. A Study In Scarlet. A Novel;** A. L. Burt, N.Y; frontis. by A. Watson Davis; red cloth, ruled border in blind; gilt; Cr. 8vo
857. **[n.d.]. A Study In Scarlet and A Case of Identity;** E. H. Weeks, Chicago; olive-brown cloth, the spine & corners in morocco-grain, the side panels in diagonal-grain cloth, separated by rules in blind; gilt; t.e.g; Cr. 8vo
858. **[n.d.]. [A Study in Scarlet] Sherlock Holmes Detective Stories;** Three Pay Sales Corporation, N.Y; reprint; frontis. photograph of the author; red cloth, ruled & pic. blocked in blind; gilt; Demy 8vo
859. **[n.d.]. [A Study In Scarlet] Sherlock Holmes. A Novel;** Ogilvie, N.Y; The Sunset Series, No. 279; pic. wrappers in black & white, depicting Sherlock Holmes in quilted dressing-gown, with pipe in the left hand, revolver in the right; 8vo

**The Surgeon of Gaster Fell [And Other Stories]**
860. **1890.** Story in: Chambers's Journal, Dec. issue
861. [*c.* **1892].** In: The Sign of the Four. A Scandal in Bohemia — And Other Stories [q.v.]
862. **[n.d; Copyright 1895].** M. J. Ivers, N.Y; 'American Series', No. 362; printed wrappers with No. 362 on spine; title story, 53 pp; The Sign of the Four [q.v.] separate pagination [3-176], is followed by 12 pp. adverts [A Piracy?]
*see also* **The Doings of Raffles Haw with The Surgeon of Gaster Fell** [q.v.]

**The Surgeon Talks**
863. **1894.** Story in: Round The Red Lamp

**Survival**
*see* **Psychic Experiences** [q.v.]

***The Sussex Vampire [The Adventure of]**
864. **1924.** Story in: The Strand Magazine, Jan. issue; illus. by Howard K. Elcock
865. **1927.** Story in: The Case-Book of Sherlock Holmes [q.v.]

**Sweethearts**
866. **1894.** Story in: The Idler Magazine, Jul. issue
867. **1894.** Story in: McClure's Magazine, Oct. issue
868. **1894.** Story in: Round The Red Lamp [q.v.]

**Take Heart**
869. **1922.** In: The Poems of Arthur Conan Doyle [q.v.]

**Tales of Long Ago**
870. **[1922].** Murray; 'Uniform Edition'; first ed; blue paper boards, pic. blocked in blind; gilt; contains some stories published for the first time; 211 pp; pic. d.w; 8vo
871. **1929.** In: The Conan Doyle Stories Omnibus [q.v.]

**Tales of the High Seas**
872. **1897.** Ih: Pearson's Magazine, Mar; May, and Jun. issues; illus. by Warwick Goble

**Tempted by the Devil**
873. **1895.** In: Cosmopolitan, Sep. issue [not in Locke]

**Terror and Mystery [Tales of]**
874. **1919.** In: The Black Doctor and Other Tales of Terror and Mystery [q.v.]
875. **[1922].** Murray; 'Uniform Edition'; first ed; blue paper boards, pic. blocked in blind; gilt; contains seven stories published for the first time; 310 pp; 8vo

**The Terror of Blue John Gap**
876. **1910.** Story in: The Strand Magazine, Aug. issue; illus. by Harry Rountree
877. **1911.** Story in: The Last Galley [q.v.]

**That Little Square Box**
878. **1889.** Story in: Mysteries and Adventures [q.v.]
879. **1890.** Story in: The Captain of the Pole-Star [q.v.]

**The Third Generation**
880. **1894.** Story in: Round The Red Lamp [q.v.]

***Thor Brige [The Problem of]**
881. **1922.** Story in: The Strand Magazine, Feb. and Mar. issues; illus. by A. Gilbert
882. **1927.** Story in: The Case-Book of Sherlock Holmes [q.v.]

**Those Others**
883. **1919.** Poem in: The Guards Came Through [q.v.]

**The Three Correspondents**
884. **1896.** Story in: The Windsor Magazine, Vol. 4, Jul.-Nov; 5 illus. by Warwick Goble, and 1 illus. by G. Montbard

***The Three Gables [The Adventure of]**
885. **1926.** Story in: The Strand Magazine, Oct. issue; illus. by Howard K. Elcock
886. **1927.** Story in: The Case-Book of Sherlock Holmes [q.v.]

***The Three Garridebs [The Adventure of]**
887. **1925.** Story in: The Strand Magazine, Jan. issue; illus. by Howard K. Elcock
888. **1927.** Story in: The Case-Book of Sherlock Holmes [q.v.]

THREE OF THEM. A REMINISCENCE
889. **1918-23.** Some of the sketches which appear in this volume appeared previously in The Strand Magazine between these years
890. **1918.** Some of the sketches in: Danger! And Other Stories [q.v.]
891. **1923.** Murray; first separate ed; frontis; grey linen boards; red linen spine; printed paper label; 99 pp; pic. d.w; 8vo

***The Three Students [The Adventure of]**
892. **1904.** Story in: The Strand Magazine, Jun. issue; illus. by Sidney Paget
893. **1905.** Story in: The Return of Sherlock Holmes [q.v.]

THROUGH THE MAGIC DOOR
894. **1906-7.** In Cassell's Magazine, Nov. 1906-Oct. 1907; illus. (serialised)
895. **1907.** Smith, Elder; first ed; 16 illus. (of which 5 are by Sir W. Russell-Flint); red cloth, pic. blocked & titled gilt; gilt lettering on spine; 274 pp; 6 pp. adverts at end; Cr. 8vo
896. **1907.** Tauchnitz Copyright Edition, Leipzig; printed wrappers; Sm. 8vo
897. **1907.** Toronto; first Canadian ed.
898. **1912.** Second Impr. of the first ed.
899. **1920.** Murray; reprint of the first ed; 16 illus; red cloth; spine gilt lettered; 274 pp; Cr. 8vo
900. [*c.* **1920**]. Nelson; pink boards; publisher's device in blind on front cover; spine titled gilt; 253 pp; 2 pp. adverts at end; Cr. 8vo

**Through the Veil**
901. **1911.** Story in: The Last Galley [q.v.]
902. **[1922].** Story in: Tales of Long Ago [q.v.]

**To Arms!**
903. **[1914].** Hodder & Stoughton; first ed; printed wrappers, stapled; poor quality newsprint; 32 pp; Cr. 8vo [scarce]

**To Carlo**
904. **1922.** In: The Poems of Arthur Conan Doyle [q.v.]

**To My Lady**
905. **1922.** In: The Poems of Arthur Conan Doyle [q.v.]

**To Ronald Ross**
906. **1922.** In: The Poems of Arthur Conan Doyle [q.v.]

**Touch and Go: A Midshipman's Story**
907. **1886.** In: Cassell's Family Magazine; illus. [not in Locke]

THE TRAGEDY OF THE KOROSKO
908. **1897.** In: The Strand Magazine; illus. by Sidney Paget (serialised)
909. **1898.** Smith, Elder; first ed; 40 illus. by Sidney Paget; red cloth; front cover pic. blocked & titled gilt; spine titled gilt; 333 pp; 6 pp. adverts at end; Cr. 8vo

[THE TRAGEDY OF THE KOROSKO] A DESERT DRAMA
910. **1898.** Lippincott, Philadelphia; first U.S. ed; 32 full-page illus. by Sidney Paget; lime-green cloth, ruled borders, titling and dec. in dark-green; Cr. 8vo (reprinted in 1905)
911. [*c.* **1906**]. Smith, Elder; New and Cheaper Edition; illus; Cr. 8vo
912. **1908.** Lippincott, Philadelphia [Higham, p. 352]
913. **1936.** Queensway Press; Chevron Books, No. 4

**The Treatment of Our Prisoners**
914. **1915.** British Government pamphlet; wrappers; 8vo

**The Truth of Spiritualism. Verbatim Report of A Public Debate between Sir Arthur Conan Doyle, M.D; Ll.D; and Joseph McCabe. Held at the Queen's Hall, London, on March 11, 1920. Revised by Both Disputants**
915. **1920.** Watts; first ed; orange cloth, bordered & titled in black; 57 pp; Demy 8vo [not in Locke]
916. **1922.** Girard, Kansas: Holdeman Julius; wrappers

**Twilight and the Unseen [Tales of]**
917. **[1922].** Murray; 'Uniform Edition'; first ed; blue paper boards, blocked pic. in blind; gilt; contains some stories published for the first time; 312 pp; 8vo
918. **1929.** In: The Conan Doyle Stories Omnibus [q.v.]

**The Two Barks**
919. **1897.** Story in: McClure's Magazine, Jul. issue
920. **[n.d.].** Story in: The Dealings of Captain Sharkey and Other Tales of Pirates [q.v.]

**The Uncharted Coast**
921. **1919-21.** In: The Strand Magazine (serialised)

UNCLE BERNAC **A Memory of the Empire**
922. **1896-7.** Issued in parts (only the first two have been located); the first dated 1896, and the second 1897; Horace Cox; grey paper wrappers; Large 4to (published at 1/- ea.)
923. **1897.** Smith, Elder; first complete ed. in book form; 12 illus. by Tauber; red fine-grain cloth; front cover & spine gilt; 300 pp; 8 pp. adverts at end; Cr. 8vo
924. **1897.** In: The Queen, Jan; Feb; and Mar. issues (serialised)
925. [*c.* **1900**]. Smith, Elder; Second Edition; Cr. 8vo
926. **1929.** Murray's Fiction Library; blue cloth; front cover pic. blocked in blind; spine dec. & titled gilt; 300 pp; 4 pp. adverts at end; Sm. 8vo
927. **1932.** In: The Conan Doyle Historical Romances Omnibus [q.v.]
928. **1934.** Murray; 'Uniform Edition'; red cloth, black lettered; 300 pp; 4 pp. adverts at end; Cr. 8vo
929. **1956.** In: The Complete Napoleonic Stories Omnibus [q.v.]

***Uncle Jeremy's Household**
930. **1887.** In: The Boy's Own Paper, Jan. 8th; Jan. 15th; Jan. 22nd; Jan. 29th; Feb. 5th, 12th and 19th; later issued in: The Boys Own Annual for 1886-7 [q.v.]
931. **1887. In: The Boy's Own Annual, vol. IX [1886-7];** illus. by R. C. W. [R. Caton Woodville]; red fine-grain cloth over bevelled boards, pic. blocked in black, titled gilt; large 8vo [The narrator of this story is a student doctor preparing for his finals, who lives in Baker Street; thus it would appear he is the precursor of Dr. Watson in *The Study in Scarlet*, written one year later] [scarce]

**The Usher of Lea House School**
*see* **The Latin Tutor** [q.v.]

*THE VALLEY OF FEAR
932. **1914-15.** In: The Strand Magazine, Sep. 1914 — May 1915 issues; illus. by Frank Wiles
933. **1914.** In: The Philadelphia Press, Sep. 6-Nov. 22; illus. by Arthur I. Keller
934. **1914.** In: Boston Sunday Post, Sep. 20-Nov. 22; illus. by Arthur I. Keller
935. **1915.** Smith, Elder; first ed; frontis. by Frank Wiles; red fine diaper-grain cloth, ruled border in blind, titled gilt on front cover and spine; 306 pp; 6 pp. adverts at end; Cr. 8vo
936. **1915.** Geo. Bell; Colonial Edition; identical to first ed; 24 pp. adverts at end; Cr. 8vo

**The Valley of Fear. A Sherlock Holmes Novel**
937. **1915.** Doran, N.Y; first U.S. ed; illus. by Arthur I. Keller; red cloth, titled gilt; 320pp; Demy 8vo
938. [**1916**]. Nelson's Continental Library, vol. 17; 286 pp; 8vo
939. [**1920**]. A. L. Burt, N.Y; 4 illus. by Arthur I. Keller; 320 pp; 8vo
940. **1922.** Murray; 306 pp; 8vo
941. [**n.d.**]. Newnes; reprint; col. pic. wrappers; 144 pp; 8vo
942. **1950. The Valley of Fear. A Sherlock Holmes Novel.** Introduction by John Dickson Carr; Bantam Books, No. 733; 181 pp; 8vo

***The Veiled Lodger [The Adventure of]**
943. **1927.** Story in: The Strand Magazine, Feb. issue; illus. by Frank Wiles
944. **1927.** Story in: The Case-Book of Sherlock Homes [q.v.]

**Victrix**
945. **1919.** Poem in: The Guards Came Through [q.v.]

**A Visit to Three Fronts**
946. **1916.** Hodder & Stoughton; white paper wrappers; blue lettering and small outline map on front cover; blue lettering on spine; 78 pp; 6 x 4¼ in.
947. [**1916**]. Doran, N.Y; first U.S. ed; 8vo

**The Vital Message**
948. [**1919**]. Hodder & Stoughton; first ed; black cloth; single ruled border in blind; gilt; 227 pp; Cr. 8vo
949. [**1924?**]. Hodder & Stoughton: tenth thou.

**The Voice of Science**
950. **1891.** In: The Strand Magazine, Mar. issue; pic. blue silk over bevelled boards; a.e.g; 4to (Royal Edition, issued in honour of Queen Victoria)
951. [**n.d.**]. In: Illustrated Penny Tales from the 'Strand Library', No. 2 (published at the Office of Tit-Bits)

**The Volunteer**
952. **1919.** Poem in: The Guards Came Through [q.v.]

**A Voyage—1909**
953. **1911.** Poem in: Songs of the Road [q.v.]

**The Voyage of Copley Banks**
954. **1897.** In: McClure's Magazine, Aug. issue
955. [**n.d.**]. Story in: The Dealings of Captain Sharkie [q.v.]

**The Wanderer**
956. **1911.** Poem in: Songs of the Road [q.v.]

THE WANDERINGS OF A SPIRITUALIST
957. [**1921**]. Hodder & Stoughton; first ed; blue fine-ribbed cloth, ruled border in blind; gilt; 316 pp; Demy 8vo
958. [*c.* **1924**]. Hodder & Stoughton; Second Edition; illus; Demy 8vo
(This is the first volume of a trilogy with Our American Adventure [q.v.] and Our Second American Adventure [q.v.] and deals with Australia and New Zealand)

**The War in South Africa. Its Cause & Conduct**
959. **1902.** Smith, Elder; first ed; printed wrappers; 156 pp; Cr. 8vo
960. **1902.** As above; New Edition; 159 pp; Cr. 8vo
961. **1902.** Morang, Toronto; first Canadian ed; 139 pp; 8vo
962. [*c.* **1902**]. Bell's Colonial Edition

**'Ware Holes!**
963. **1898.** Poem in: Songs of Action [q.v.]

WESTERN WANDERINGS
964. **1915.** In: The Cornhill Magazine, Jan.-Apr. issues; printed wrappers; Demy 8vo
965. **1915.** Doran, N.Y; first U.S. ed; 8vo

**W. G. Grace [A Memory]**
966. **1927.** In: The Strand Magazine

**What Does Spiritualism Actually Teach and Stand For?**
967. **[1928]**. Psychic Press; wrappers; 16 pp; 8vo

**When The World Screamed**
968. **1928.** In: The Strand Magazine
969. **1928.** [Locke, p. 78: "A book edition of this story which also appeared in The Strand Magazine in the early part of this present year [1928] is also in the press]
970. **1952.** In: The Professor Challenger Stories Omnibus [q.v.]

THE WHITE COMPANY
971. **1891.** In: The Cornhill Magazine, Jan.-Dec. issues (serialised)
972. **1891.** Smith, Elder; first ed; red-brown cloth; black lettering and design on front cover; gilt lettering on spine, with design in black; flowered e.p.s; 3 vols: vol. I, 311 pp; vol. II, 302 pp; vol. III, 277 pp; Cr. 8vo [scarce]
973. [*c.* **1893**]. Tauchnitz Copyright Edition, Leipzig; 2 vols; Sm. 8vo‡
974. [*c.* **1894**]. Harper & Bros; N.Y; illus. by George Willis Bardwell; dark-blue cloth, pic. blocked & titled gilt; Cr. 8vo
975. [*c.* **1896**]. Fenno, N.Y; light-blue cloth, front cover & spine dec. & titled white; Cr. 8vo
976. **1900.** Smith, Elder; New and Cheaper Edition; 8 illus; 416 pp; 8vo
977. **1901.** Newnes' Sixpenny Copyright series; 222 pp; Sm. 8vo
978. [*c.* **1902**]. Appleton, N.Y; illus; limp morocco, ruled gilt; t.e.g; Demy 8vo
979. [*c.* **1906**]. Smith, Elder; 8 illus; 28th ed; Cr. 8vo
980. **1918.** Murray, reprint of first ed.
981. **1926.** Murray; School Edition; red cloth, titled black, front cover & spine; 370 pp; 1 p. advert at end; Sm. 8vo (reprinted 1927)
982. **1931.** In: The Conan Doyle Historical Romances Omnibus [q.v.]
983. **1968.** Murray; paperback; pic. cover; 370 pp; 8vo
984. **1975.** Murray & Cape; intro. by Anthony Burgess; first ed. thus; 441 pp; pic. d.w. by Leigh Taylor; 8vo
985. **[n.d.]**. Rand, McNally, Chicago; 'Alpha Library' ed; green fine-ribbed cloth, ruled & dec. panel, all in blind & titled gilt; Cr. 8vo ‡[Locke, p. 33, says that at the time of writing [1928], 50 editions had been published and that all subsequent editions to the first were in one volume]

**Who Carries the Gun?**
986. **1928.** In: The Collected Poems of Arthur Conan Doyle [q.v.], Doyle mentions in his Preface, dated June 1928, that this poem has been included in this volume. It has, in fact, been omitted!

**Who Wrote The Letters?**
987. **1907.** Articles in: The Daily Telegraph re the Edalji case; *see also* **The Case of Mr. George Edalji** (q.v.]

**Why He Is Now In Favour Of Home Rule**
988. **1911.** Liberal Publications Dept; 2 pp. leaflet, dated 26/9/11; Cr. 8vo

**The Wild Geese. The Story of the Irish Brigades in France**
989. **1954.** In: The Irish Times, 13-22 Sep. [MS dating from the end of 1897 or beginning of 1898]

***Wisteria Lodge [The Adventure of]**
990. **1908.** Story in: The Strand Magazine, Sep. issue; illus. by Arthur Twidle
991. **1917.** Story in: His Last Bow [q.v.]

**With the Chiddingfolds**
992. **1898.** Poem in: Songs of Action [q.v.]

**A Woman's Love**
993. **1911.** Poem in: Songs of the Road [q.v.]

**A Word of Warning**
994. **[1928]**. The Psychic Press; first ed; printed wrappers; 19 pp; 8vo

**A Worker of Wonders**
995. **1921.** In: The Strand Magazine

**The Wreck of Loch McGarry**
996. **1919.** Poem in: The Guards Came Through [q.v.]

***The Yellow Face [The Adventure of]**
997. **1893.** Story in: The Strand Magazine, Feb. issue; illus. by Sidney Paget
998. **1894.** Story in: The Memoirs of Sherlock Holmes [q.v.]

**"Ypres" [September 1915]**
999. **1919.** Poem in: The Guards Came Through [q.v.]
1000. **[1928]**. Poem in: The Queen's Gift Book [q.v. item 1035]

**An Amazing Seance and An Exposure. By Sidney A. Mosley, with an Introduction by Sir Arthur Conan Doyle**
1001. **1919.** Sampson, Low; first ed; illus; buff-brown cloth, ruled borders and titled in black; Cr. 8vo [not in Locke]

**Brave Deeds by Brave Men. By C. Sheridan Jones. Foreword by Sir A. Conan Doyle**
1002. **[1924].** Raphael Tuck; first ed; illus. in colour by Howard Davie and Harry Payne; pic. glazed boards printed in full colours; linen spine, titled black; boxed (same illustration on lid as on front cover); Cr. 4to [not in Locke]

**The British Legion Album.** (Contains a facsimile of the MS of a chapter from Doyle's History of the Great War — the last chapter with his signature)
1003. [*c.* **1918**]. Cassell; first ed; printed & dec. wrappers, cut flush, col. illus. superimposed; 8vo [not in Locke]

**The Case For And Against Psychical Belief. Edited by Carl Murchison. Contributors include: Sir Olver Lodge, Houdini. etc.** (Contains Chapter 2 by Doyle, entitled; The Psychic Question As I See It)
1004. **1927.** Clark University, Worcester, Mass; first ed; red fine-ribbed cloth, borders in blind, titled gilt; 8vo [not in Locke]

**The Case of Lester Coltman. With a Preface by Sir A. C. Doyle**
1005. **1923.** Hutchinson

***A Century of Thrillers From Poe to Arlen. With a Foreword by James Agate.** (Contains The Adventure of The Speckled Band)
1006. **1934.** Daily Express Publications; first ed; cloth, pic. blocked & titled black; Demy 8vo

***Century of Thrillers** (Contains The Adventure of The Speckled Band and The Adventure of The Blue Carbuncle)
1007. **[1937].** President Press, N.Y; first ed; red cloth, pic. blocked & titled black; 3 vols; Cr. 8vo

**The Construction and Reconstruction of the Human Body. By E. Sandow. Foreword by Sir A. Conan Doyle**
1008. **1907.** [Nordon, p. 350; not in Locke]

**D. D. Home. His Life and Mission. By Madame Douglas Home. Edited and with a Preface by Sir Arthur Conan Doyle**
1009. **1921.** Kegan Paul; first ed; maroon net-grain cloth, ruled border in blind, gilt; d.w. containing Doylian blurb; 8vo [Incorrectly entered by Locke, p.23, as 'Life of D. D. Home']

***The Detective in Fiction, A Posse of Eight. Selected from the stories of well-known writers and introduced by E. A. Seaborne** (Contains (———) Silver Blaze)
1010. **1931.** Bell; first ed; cloth, titled in black; 8vo

**Divorce and Morality. By C. S. Bremmer. Preface by Sir Arthur Conan Doyle**
1011. **1912.** [Nordon, p. 350]

**The Evolution of Spiritualism. By Harvey Metcalfe. With a Preface by Sir Arthur Conan Doyle**
1012. **1924.** [Publisher?]

**Famous Crimes, Mysteries & Romances. The Great Stories of Real Life. Contributors include: Edgar Wallace, George Blake, etc.** (Contains The Strange Case of George Edalji & The Case of Oscar Slater — [q.v.]
1013. **[n.d.].** Newnes; illus; black morocco-grain cloth; labels; bound up from monthly parts; set of 4 vols; 4to

**The Fate of Fanella. By Helen Mathers, Mrs. Trollope, A. Conan Doyle & Others**
1014. **1892.** Hutchinson; first ed; buff cloth, dec. with facsimile signatures of all the authors involved; blocked in brown on front covers; spines titled gilt; 3 vols; Cr. 8vo [not in Locke]

**'G. H. Darby', Captain of Wyrley Gang. By G. A. Atkinson. Preface by Sir Arthur Conan Doyle**
1015. **1914.** [Nordon, p. 250 — not in Locke]

**Glorious Battles of English History. By Major C. H. Wylly. Foreword by Sir Arthur Conan Doyle**
1016. **[1924?].** Raphael Tuck; first ed; 12 full-page illus. by Harry Payne and numerous illus. in b. & w; cloth-backed pic. boards in full colours; 144 pp; boxed (same illus. on lid as on front cover); Cr. 4to [not in Locke]

**Great Britain and the Congo. By E. D. Morel. Introduction by Sir Arthur Conan Doyle**
1017. **1909.** [Nordon, p. 350 — not in Locke]

***The Great Detectives** (Contains The Adventure of The Crooked Man)
1018. **[1947].** Hennel Locke; first ed; light-blue cloth, pic. blocked in dark-blue; Cr. 8vo

**Hilda Wade. By Grant Allen**
1019. **1900.** Grant Allen; first ed; illus. by Gordon Browne; dark-blue cloth, pic. blocked & titled gilt; t.e.g; Sq. Cr. 8vo [Doyle has confessed to having partially written this novel. An autograph letter exists in which he makes this statement — not in Locke]

**I Escape. By Captain J. L. Hardie, D.S.O; M.C. Introduction by Sir Arthur Conan Doyle**
1020. **[1927].** Cherry Tree Books; first ed; col. pic. wrappers, cut flush; 8vo [Locke has it as 'Captain J. L. Hardy', and published by The Bodley Head Press]

**If I Were A Preacher — A Symposium. Contributors include: G. K. Chesterton. Bertrand Russell, etc.** (Contains Doyle's 'The Religion of the Future')
1021. **[1929].** Cassell; first ed; red cloth, ruled borders in blind; spine titled in black; Cr. 8vo

**Life After Death. By J. M. Wilson, Canon of Worcester. With replies by Sir A. Conan Doyle**
1022. **1920.** [Not in Locke]

**The Life Beyond the Veil. Spirit Messages received & written down by the Rev. G. Vale Owen. Introduction by Sir Arthur Conan Doyle**
1023. **1919.** Butterworth, first ed; maroon cloth, spine titled in black; Cr. 8vo

**Modern Anglo-Irish Verse — An Anthology Selected from the Work of Living Irish Poets. Contributors include: James Joyce, Lord Dunsany, Yeats, etc.** (Contains Doyle's poems 'Cremona' [q.v.] and 'The Irish Colonel' [q.v.]
1024. **1914.** David Nutt; first ed; olive-green cloth, ruled border & dec. in blind, titled gilt; Cr. 8vo

**My First Book. Contributors include: Kipling, R. L. Stevenson. etc.** (Contains Doyle's 'Juvenilia' [q.v.])
1025. **1897.** Chatto & Windus; New Edition; 185 illus; red cloth, dec. & titled in black, silver & gilt; Cr. 8vo

**My Religion — A Symposium. By Sir Arthur Conan Doyle, Arnold Bennett, Hugh Walpole, Rebecca West and Other Authors**
1026. [*c.* **1926**]. Hutchinson; first ed; grey cloth, ruled border in blind on front cover; spine titled in black; Cr. 8vo [not in Locke]

***The Mystery Book. Edited by H. Douglas Thomson** (Contains The Adventure of The Speckled Band)
1027. **[1934].** Odhams Press; first ed; black cloth, pic. blocked & titled gilt; Demy 8vo

**The Mystery of Joan of Arc. By Leon Denis. Translated from the French and with a Preface by A. Conan Doyle**
1028. **[1924].** Murray; first ed; 8 illus; light-blue cloth; front cover & spine titled gilt; 233 pp; 8 pp. adverts at end; 8vo

**One-Act Plays of Today — Second Series. Selected by J. W. Marriott** (Contains Doyle's [The Story of] Waterloo [q.v.])
1029. **1925.** Harrap; first ed; olive-green cloth, blocked & titled in darker green; 267 pp; Sm. 8vo (reprinted 1926 once; 1927 twice)

**Peril & Prowse. Stories by A. Conan Doyle, G. A. Henty, W. W. Jacobs & Others** (Contains The Mystery of Sasassa Valley [q.v.])
1030. **1899.** Chambers; first ed; 8 illus. by W. Boucher; red cloth over bevelled boards; pic. blocked & titled in black & green; Cr. 8vo [not in Locke]

**Phantoms of the Dawn. By Violet Tweedale. Foreword by Sir Arthur Conan Doyle**
1031. **[1924].** Long; Second Impr; cloth; spine titled in blind; Cr. 8vo [not in Locke]
1032. **[1938?].** [Publisher?]; Cheap Edition; pic. wrappers, cut flush; duplicate pic. d.w; 8vo

**The Press Album**
*see* item 102

**Princess Mary's Gift Book. Contributors include: H. Rider Haggard, Kipling, A. E. W. Mason, etc.** (Contains Bimbashi Joyce [q.v.])
1033. [*c.* **1919**]. Hodder & Stoughton; illus. in col. and b. & w; Sm. 4to [not in Locke]

**Psychic Experiences of A Musician. By von Reuter. With a Preface by Sir A. C. Doyle**
1034. **1928.** The Psychic Press

**The Queen's Gift Book. Contributors include: E. F. Benson, John Buchan, etc.** (Contains Doyle's poem "Ypres" [q.v.]; illus. with drawings by L. Raven-Hill)
1035. **[1928].** Hodder & Stoughton; first ed; tipped-in col. illus. & drawings in b. & w. by various artists; blue cloth; Sm. 4to

**Rosemary. Compiled by F. De Burgh and Walter Stoneman** (Contains The Lord of Falconbridge [q.v.], together with a portrait of Sir Arthur Conan Doyle)
1036. **[1924].** Sampson Low; first ed; 21 camera portraits; blue buckram, gilt; Demy 8vo

**Six Complete Stories from Lippincott** (Contains The Sign of the Four [q.v.])
1037. **1890.** Ward, Lock; first ed; light-blue cloth; gilt design on front cover & spine; chocolate-col. e.p.s; 4to

**The Souvenir of the Charing Cross Hospital Bazaar held at the Albert Hall, June 21 & 22. Compiled & Edited by Herbert Beerbohm Tree. Contributors include: Max Beerbohm, Anthony Hope, Pinero, etc.** (Contains Doyle's Poem 'A Soldier's Prayer' with a photograph)
1038. **1899.** Nassau Press & Virtue; each contribution is accompanied by a photograph of the author & a facsimile of their autograph; dec. boards; linen spine; Folio

**Spiritualism. Its History, Phenomena, & Doctrine. By J. Arthur Hill. With an Introduction by Sir Arthur Conan Doyle**
1039. **1918.** Cassell; first ed; grey cloth, titled on front cover in blue; spine gilt; Cr. 8vo

**The Sunlight Year Book**
*see* item 100

**Strange Stories of Coincidence & Ghostly Adventure.** (Contains J. Habakuk Jephson's Statement [q.v.] and 9 other stories by anonymous authors)
1040. **[1891].** Geo. Redway; first ed; light-blue cloth, with a frosted pattern & ruled borders in blind; gilt; Cr. 8vo

**A Symposium on Books & Other Things by Famous Writers of Today. Edited by H. Greenhough** (Contains Doyle's "How I Write My Books"; "The Book I Most Enjoyed Writing", & "What I Think")
1041. **[n.d.].** Newnes; John O'London's Little Books, No. 9; frontis; green boards, pic. blocked & titled in black; 8vo [not in Locke]

**The Truth About Oscar Slater — With the Prisoner's Own Story. By William Park. With A Statement by Sir Arthur Conan Doyle**
1042. **[1927].** The Psychic Press; first ed; cloth, gilt; Cr. 8vo

**The Undiscovered Country. A Sequence of Spirit Messages describing Death & The After-World. Selected from Published and Unpublished Automatic Writings. 1874-1918. Edited by Harold Bayley. With an Introduction by Sir Arthur Conan Doyle**
1043. **1918.** Cassell; first ed; bistre-brown buckram; printed label; Cr. 8vo

***The Adventures of Sherlock Holmes; The Later Adventures of Sherlock Holmes, and The Final Adventures of Sherlock Holmes. A definitive text, corrected and edited by Edgar W. Smith. With an Introduction by Vincent Starrett**
1044. **1950.** The Heritage Press, N.Y; first ed; illus. by Sidney Paget, Frederic Dorr Steele, & Others; three-quarter dec. boards; black linen spines; gilt; Demy 8vo; 3 vols. boxed in a black slip-case
1045. **1952.** As above; Limited Editions Club; Adventures (3 vols.); Later Adventures (3 vols.) Final Adventures (2 vols.); together 8 vols.; glassine wrappers; boxed in 3 slip-cases

***"Author's Edition". The Collected Edition of Sir A. Conan Doyle's Novels. With an Introductory Preface**
1046. **1903.** Smith, Elder; 2 photogravure illus. in each vol; the first vol. (The White Company) being signed by the author and numbered; cloth, gilt; Demy 8vo; 12 vols; limited edition of 1,000 sets [It may be of interest to know that this set was advertised at "6/- each net" — it was actually sold in sets only, for £3.12 net per set] (An edition-de-luxe was published in the U.S.A.)

**The Complete Napoleonic Stories Omnibus** (Contains: Uncle Bernac; Exploits of Brigadier Gerard; Adventures of Gerard, & The Great Shadow)
1047. **1956.** Murray; first ed. in one vol; red cloth, titled in black; pic. d.w; thick Cr. 8vo

***The Complete Sherlock Holmes**
1048. **1930.** Doubleday, Doran & Co; N.Y; first ed; 2 vols.
1049. **1936.** As above; one-vol. ed.

***The Complete Sherlock Holmes. The A. Conan Doyle Memorial Edition. With a Preface by Christopher Morley**
1050. **1930.** Doubleday, N.Y; black cloth, titled red; Cr. 8vo; 2-vol. ed.

***The Complete Sherlock Holmes Long Stories Omnibus** (Contains: A Study In Scarlet; The Sign of Four; The Hound of the Baskervilles, and The Valley of Fear)
1051. **1929.** Murray; first ed. in one vol; red cloth, titled black; pic. d.w; thick Cr. 8vo

***The Complete Sherlock Holmes Short Stories Omnibus** (Contains all the stories from The Adventures, The Memoirs, The Return, The Case-Book of Sherlock Holmes, and His Last Bow)
1052. **1928.** Murray; preface by Conan Doyle to this edition, dated 1928; first ed. in one vol; red cloth, titled black; pic. d.w; thick Cr. 8vo

***Conan Doyle's Best Books. Sherlock Holmes Edition**
1053. **[n.d.].** Collier, N.Y; illus; cloth; portrait blocks on front covers & spines; gilt; Demy 8vo; 3-vol. ed.

**The Conan Doyle Historical Romances Omnibus** (Contains: vol. I: The White Company; Sir Nigel; Micah Clarke; The Refugees; vol. II: Rodney Stone; Uncle Bernac; Adventures of Gerard; Exploits of Brigadier Gerard)
1054. **1931-2.** Murray; preface by Jean Conan Doyle in vol. I, dated 1931; first ed. in 2 vols; red cloth, titled black; pic. d.w; thick Cr. 8vo

**The Conan Doyle Stories Omnibus** (Contains: Tales of The Ring and the Camp; Pirates and Blue Water; Terror and Mystery; Twilight and the Unseen; Adventures and Medical Life, and Tales of Long Ago)
1055. **1929.** Murray; first ed. in one vol; red cloth, titled black; pic. d.w; thick Cr. 8vo

**Mysteries and Adventures Omnibus, bound up with: Oak-Bough and Wattle-Blossom. Stories and Sketches of Australians in England. Edited by A. Patchett Martin, 1888**
1056. **[1889].** Walter Scott; first ed; publisher's red cloth over bevelled boards; dec. in black; titled gilt; 12 mo [not in Locke]

**The Professor Challenger Stories Omnibus** (Contains: The Lost World; The Poison Belt; The Land of Mist; The Disintegration Machine, and When The World Screamed)
1057. **1952.** Murray, first ed. in one vol; red cloth, titled black; pic. d.w; thick Cr. 8vo

**Thin Paper Edition of the Works of Arthur Conan Doyle**
1058. **1924.** Murray; 12 vols. (a further 6 vols. followed); red fine-grain cloth; author's initials on front cover, gilt; spine dec. & titled gilt; Sm. 8vo (This edition was also published bound in red leather)

***A Treasury of Sherlock Holmes. Selected and with an Introduction by Adrian Conan Doyle**
1059. **1955.** Hanover House, N.Y; first ed; black cloth; yellow cloth spine; 686 pp; d.w; 8vo

***The Works of Conan Doyle — One-Volume Edition**
1060. **[n.d.].** Collier, N.Y; frontis; blue cloth over limp boards; author's facsimile signature blocked in gilt; spine dec. & titled gilt; t.e.g; (printed in double column)

**'Uniform Edition' of Arthur Conan Doyle's Principal Works of Fiction**
1061. **1913.** Smith, Elder; red cloth; 20 vols; 8vo
1062. **1931.** Murray; red cloth; 37 vols; 8vo (reprinted: 1935, 1947 & 1949)

1063. THE STRAND MAGAZINE

A monthly periodical founded by Geo. Newnes of London in 1891. Conan Doyle contributed fairly regularly to this magazine, from the first issue (A Scandal in Bohemia), till his death in 1930.

**Single issues:** pic. wrappers; illus; Demy 8vo

**Bound-up vols.** (6-monthly): light-blue cloth over bevelled boards; pic. blocked in black with the 'Strand Library' motif [*see* the back cover of this Bibliography] depicting The Strand, the home of the publishers — which is also found on some of the early Doyle editons published by Newnes; illus; Demy 8vo

[The earlier volumes of The Strand Magazine, which contain the original Sherlock Holmes stories, are more readily available than the later ones, whose print run was much reduced, and they are therefore very scarce]

CONAN DOYLE

# BIOGRAPHIES & CRITICAL WRITINGS

CONAN DOYLE

1064. Bates (H.E.), *The Creator of Sherlock Holmes, Sir Arthur Conan Doyle. The Man and His Books — A Critical Appreciation*, in: *The World's Great Books in Outline*, ed. by J. A. Hammerton (part 24), London 1926

1065. Brown (Ivor), *Conan Doyle*, Hamish Hamilton, London 1972

1066. Carr (John Dickson), *The Life of Sir Arthur Conan Doyle*, illus; John Murray, London 1949 and Harper & Bros; N.Y. 1949

1067. Conan Doyle (Adrian M.), *The True Conan Doyle*, with a preface by Sir Hubert Gough, John Murray, London 1945, and Coward-McCann, N.Y. 1946

1068. Conan Doyle (Adrian M.), and P. Weil-Nordon (Ed.), *Sir Arthur Conan Doyle Centenary* 1859-1959, John Murray, London 1959 and Doubleday, N.Y. n.d. [An illustrated commemorative album]

1069. Cooke, (Ivan) (Ed.), *The Return of Sir Arthur Conan Doyle*, The White Eagle Publishing Trust, Hampshire 1956

1070. Cromwell (Archibald), *Dr. Conan Doyle and His Stories: A Pen Portrait of the Author*, illus. by H. C. Sepping-Wright and Arthur Cooke, in: The Windsor Magazine, vol. 4, Jul.-Nov. 1896

1071. *A Day With Conan Doyle*, in: The Strand Magazine, Aug. 1892 issue

1072. Ernst (Bernard M. L.), and Hereward Carrington, *Houdini and Conan Doyle, The Story of a Strange Friendship*. Foreword by J. C. Cannell, Hutchinson, London 1933

1073. Hatch (Robert), *The Real Conan Doyle*, illus. after originals of Sidney Paget, in: The Idler, vol. i, No. 2, Feb. 1967

1074. Higham (Charles), *The Adventures of Conan Doyle, The Creator of Sherlock Holmes*, illus; Hamish Hamilton, London 1976

1075. Kittle (C. Frederick), *Arthur Conan Doyle, Doctor and Writer* (1859-1930), reprinted from the Journal of the Kensas Medical Soc; vol. LXI, No. 1, pp. 13-18, Jan. 1960

1076. Lamond (J.), *Arthur Conan Doyle, A Memoir: with an Epilogue by Lady Conan Doyle*, John Murray, London 1931

1077. Locke (H.), *A Bibliographical Catalogue of the Writings of Sir Arthur Conan Doyle*, 1879-1928. Tunbridge Wells 1928

1078. Maclauchlan (Hugh S.), *Dr. Conan Doyle and His Stories: An Appreciation of His Work:* illus. by H. C. Sepping-Wright and Arthur Cooke, in: The Windsor Magazine, vol. 4, Jul.-Nov. 1896

1079. Nordon (Pierre), *Conan Doyle*, transl. from the French by Frances Partridge, illus; John Murray, London 1966

1080. Pearsall (Ronald), *Conan Doyle — A Biographical Solution*, illus; Weidenfeld & Nicolson, London 1977

1081. Pearson (Hesketh), *Conan Doyle, His Life and Art*, illus; Methuen, London 1943

1082. Raymond (E.T.), *All and Sundry*, Fisher Unwin, London (1919) [One chapter on Conan Doyle]

1083. Tweedale (Charles L.), *News from the Next World*, T. Werner Laurie, London 1940 [Chapt. VIII: Conan Doyle Joins, 5 illus.]

SHERLOCK HOLMES

# HOLMESIANA

SHERLOCK HOLMES

*For Further titles the reader is recommended to refer to:*

1084. *The World Bibliography of Sherlock Holmes and Dr. Watson by Robert Burt de Waal*, New York Graphic Society, Boston 1974

1085. Baring-Gould (William S.), *The Chronological Holmes*, privately printed, N.Y. 1955

1086. Baring-Gould (William S.), *Sherlock Holmes, A Biography of the World's First Consulting Detective*, Hart Davis, London 1962

1087. Baring-Gould (William S.) (Ed.), *The Annotated Sherlock Holmes*. John Murray, London 1968

1088. Bell (H.W.) (Ed.), *Baker Street Studies*, Constable, London 1934

1089. Bell (H.W.), *Sherlock Holmes and Dr. Watson: The Chronology of Their Adventures*. Constable, London 1932

1090. Bell (Joseph), *The Adventures of Sherlock Holmes*, in: *The Bookman*, 3 Dec. 1892

1091. Blakeney (T.S.), *Sherlock Holmes: Fact or Fiction*? John Murray, London 1932

1092. Boukhov (A.), *The End of Sherlock Holmes*, in: Dekobra (Maurice), *The Crimson Smile* (*Le Rive dans la Steppe*), transl. from the French by Metcalfe Wood, Werner Laurie, London 1929 (not in World Bibliography)

1093. Brend (Gavin), *My Dear Holmes*, Allen & Unwin, London 1951

1094. Carr (John Dickson), *The Valley of Fear, A Sherlock Holmes Novel*, Introduction by John Dickson Carr, Bantam Books, No. 733; 181 pp; London 1950

1095. Christ (Jay Finley), *An Irregular Guide to Sherlock Holmes of Baker Street*, Argus Books, New York 1947

1096. Cutter (Robert A.) (Ed.), *Sherlockian Studies: Seven Pieces of Sherlockiana*, The Baker Street Press, N.Y. 1947

1097. Conan Doyle (Adrian M.), and John Dickson Carr, *The Exploits of Sherlock Holmes*, John Murray, London 1954; also available in paperback, 2 vols.

1098. Conan Doyle (Adrian M.), and John Dickson Carr, *More Exploits of Sherlock Holmes*, John Murray, London 1954 (reprinted 1964)

1099. Dakin (D. Martin), *A Sherlock Holmes Commentary*, David & Charles, Newton Abbot 1972

1100. *The Field Bazaar: A Sherlock Holmes Pastiche*, in: *The Student*, Edinburgh, Nov. 20 issue, and Pamphlet House, Summit, N.J. 1947

1101. Gillette (William), *The Painful Predicament of Sherlock Holmes. A Fantasy in One Act*, Ben Abramson, Chicago 1955

1102. Gillette (William), *Sherlock Holmes — A Play, based on Sir Arthur Conan Doyle's Incomparable Stories, with an Introduction by Vincent Starrett, a preface to this edition by William Gillette and Reminiscent Notes by Frederick Dorr Steele;* illus. with line drawings by Frederick Dorr Steele, Helan Halbach, Santa Barbara, California 1947 (reprint of Sherlock Holmes — A Play, [q.v.]

1103. Grazebrook (O.F.), *Studies in Sherlock Holmes*, privately printed, London 1949

1104. Greene (Grahame) (Intro.), *The Sign of Four*. John Murray, London 1974

1105. Greene (Sir Hugh), *The Rivals of Sherlock Holmes*, The Bodley Head, London 1970, and Pantheon Books, N.Y. 1970

1106. Greene (Sir Hugh), *More Rivals of Sherlock Holmes*, Cosmopolitan Crimes, 1971 and Penguin, London 1973

1107. Hall (T.H.), *Sherlock Holmes: Ten Literary Studies*, Duckworth, London 1969

1108. Hardwick (Michael and Mollie), *Sherlock Holmes Investigates*, illus. by Sidney Paget, John Murray, London 1972

1109. Hardwick (Michael and Mollie), *The Man Who Was Sherlock Holmes*, John Murray, London 1964

1110. Hardwick (Michael and Mollie), *The Sherlock Holmes Companion*, illus. by Sidney Paget, John Murray, London 1962

1111. Harrison (Michael), *Theatrical Mr. Holmes*, Covent Garden Press, London 1974 (wrappers)

1112. Harrison (Michael), *The World of Sherlock Holmes*, illus; Muller, London 1973

1113. Harrison (Michael), *In the Footsteps of Sherlock Holmes*, illus; Cassell, London 1958; Revised Edition: David & Charles, Newton Abbot 1971

1114. Holroyd (James Edward) (Ed.), *Seventeen Steps to 221B: A Collection of Sherlockian Pieces by English Writers*, with an Introduction by James Edward Holroyd, Allen & Unwin, London 1967

1115. Holroyd (James Edward), *Baker Street By-Ways. A Book About Sherlock Holmes;* illus; Allen & Unwin, London 1959

1116. Leblanc (Maurice), *Arsene Lupin versus Sherlock Holmes*. Translated from the French by Olive Harper, J. S. Ogilvie, N.Y. n.d.

1117. Lehmann (R.C.), *The Adventures of Picklock Holes, Together with a Perversion and a Burlesque*, illus. by E. T. Reed and E. J. Wheeler, Bradbury & Agnew, London 1910

1118. Lucas (E.V.) (Ed.), *The Book of the Queen's Dolls' House Library* together with *The Book of the Queen's Dolls' House*, contains: 'How Watson Learned The Trick', Methuen, London 1924, 2 vols.

1119. Marsh (Brian A.), *The Adventures of Sherlock Holmes*, introduced by Brian A. Marsh; illus. by Paul Hogarth, The Folio Society, London 1958, reprinted 1960

1120. Meyer (Nicholas), *The Seven-Per-Cent Solution — Being A Reprint from the Reminiscences of John H. Watson, M.D.*, Hodder & Stoughton, London 1975, and Companion Book Club, Feltham 1976

1121. Meyer (Nicholas), *The West End Horror — A Posthumous Memoir of John H. Watson, M.D.*, Ballantyne Books, Random House, N.Y. 1977 (paperback — previously published in hardback)

1122. Morgan (Robert S.), *Spotlight on a Simple Case, or, Wiggins, Who Was That Horse I Saw With You Last Night*? Wilmington, Delaware 1959

1123. Morley (Christopher) (Ed.), *Sherlock Holmes and Dr. Watson*, Harcourt, Brace & Co; N.Y. 1944

1124. Nathan (L. Bengis), *The 'Signs' of Our Times, An Irregular Bibliography*, N.Y. 1956 (A Bibliography of the Sign of the Four)

1125. Officer (Harvey), *A Baker Street Song Book*, The Pamphlet House, N.J. 1943

1126. Park (Orlando), *Sherlock Holmes, Esq; and John Watson, M.D; An Encyclopedia of Their Affairs*, Northwestern Univ. Press, U.S.A. 1962

1127. Petersen (Sven), *A Sherlock Holmes Almanac*, Washington D.C. 1956 (privately printed)

1128. Pointer (Michael), *The Sherlock Holmes File*, illus; David & Charles, Newton Abbot 1976

1129. Pointer (Michael), *The Public Life of Sherlock Holmes*, Drake, N.Y. 1975

1130. Queen (Ellery), *Sherlock Holmes versus Jack the Ripper. A Novel*, Gollancz, London 1967

1131. Queen (Ellery), *The Misadventures of Sherlock Holmes*, Little, Brown; Boston 1946

1132. Roberts (Sir S.C.), *Holmes & Watson — A Miscellany*, Oxford University Press, London 1953

1133. Roberts (Sir S.C.), (Ed.), *Sherlock Holmes — Selected Stories*, With an Introduction by S.C. Roberts, Worlds Classics series, Oxford University Press 1951, pic. d.w., (reprinted 1952)

1134. Roberts (Sir S.C.), *Doctor Watson: Prelogomena to the Study of q Biographical Problem, with a Bibliography of Sherlock Holmes*, Faber & Faber, London 1931

1135. Sayers (Dorothy L.), *Studies in Sherlock Holmes*, in: *Unpopular Opinions*, Gollancz, London 1946

1136. *Sherlock Holmes. Catalogue of an Exhibition*. Public Libraries Committee, St. Marylebone, London 1951

1137. Simpson (A. Carson), *Simpson's Sherlockian Studies*, illus; Philadelphia 1953-60 (privately printed)

1138. Smith (Edgar W.), *The Napoleon of Crime*, Pamphlet House, N.J. 1963 (The life of Dr. James Moriarty)

1139. Smith (Edgar W.), *Baker Street Inventory. A Sherlockian Bibliography*, Pamphlet House, Summit, N.J. 1945

1140. Smith (Edgar W.), *Letters from Baker Street*, Pamphlet House, N.Y. 1942

1141. Smith (Edgar W.), *Profile By Gaslight, An Irregular Reader about the Private Life of Sherlock Holmes*, illus; Simon & Schuster, N.Y. 1944

1142. Smith (Edgar W.), *The Heritage Sherlock Holmes*, The Heritage Press, N.Y. 1957

1143. Smith (Sir Sidney), 'Dr. Bell & Sherlock Holmes' in: *Mostly Murder*, with a Foreword by The Hon. Lord Cameron, Harrap, London (1959) & Companion Book Club, London 1961

1144. Starrett (Vincent), *The Private Life of Sherlock Holmes*, Macmillan, N.Y. 1933 and Nicholson & Watson 1934; Revised and Enlarged Edition: Allen & Unwin, London 1961

1145. Titus (Eve), *Basil of Baker Street*, illus. by Paul Galdone, N.Y. 1958 (originally pulished by McGraw-Hill, *c.* 1918) [A children's book]

1146. Todd (Peter), *The Adventures of Herlock Sholmes*, introduced by Philip Jose Farmer, The Mysteries Press, N.Y. 1976

1147. Tupper Bigelow (S.), *An Irregular Anglo-American Glossary of More or Less Unfamiliar Words, Terms and Phrases in The Sherlock Holmes Saga*, Castalotte & Zamba, Toronto 1959

1148. Van Liere (Edward J.), *A Doctor Enjoys Sherlock Holmes*, Vantage Press, N.Y. 1960

1149. Warrack (Guy), *Sherlock Holmes and Music*, Faber & Faber, London 1947

1150. Wooldridge (Clifton R.), *The American Sherlock Holmes. A Whirl of Mystery in Real Life*, illus; Laird & Lee, Chicago (1913)

1151. Wolff (Julian), *The Sherlockian Atlas*, N.Y. 1952 (privately printed)

1152. Wolff (Julian), *Practical Handbook of Sherlockian Heraldry*, N.Y. 1955 (privately printed)

1153. Zeisler (Ernest Bloomfield), *Baker Street Chronology: Commentaries on the Sacred Writings of Dr. John H. Watson*, Alexander J. Isaacs, Chicago 1953

**Journals**

1154. *The Baker Street Journal* (*Old Series*) [a quarterly]
Jan. 1946-Jan. 1949, Ben Abramson (for the Baker Street Irregulars), 13 issues, illus. (edited by Edgar W. Smith)

1155. *The Baker Street Journal* (*New Series*) [a quarterly]
Jan. 1951- Dec. 1971, The Baker Street Irregulars, Morristown, N.J; 84 issues, illus. (edited by Edgar W. Smith 1951-60; by Julian Wolff, 1961-)

1156. *The Baker Street Journal Christmas Annual*
Nos. 1-5; The Baker Street Irregulars, Morristown, N.J; 5 issues. illus; (edited by Edgar W. Smith)

1157. *The Baker Street Gasogene* [a quarterly]
1961-2. N.Y; illus; (ed. by Peter A. Ruber)

1158. *The Sherlock Holmes Journal* [biannual]
May 1952-Summer 1972; Sherlock Holmes Society of London; 40 issues, illus. (edited by The Marquess of Donegall)

# WHAT THE PRESS SAID

**A Study in Scarlet [1888]**

"Without exception the finest detective narrative which has ever been written." — **Sheffield Telegraph**

"Few things have been so good of late as Dr. Doyle's 'Study in Scarlet.' — **Andrew Lang**

"As entrancing a tale of ingenuity in tracing out crime as has been written since the time of Edgar Allan Poe." — **Scotsman**

"Everything that prince of amateur detectives, Mr. Sherlock Holmes, says is worth hearing." — **Black and White**

"A scientific detective, to whom Edgar Allan Poe's Dupin was a trifler, and Gaboriau's Lecoq a child." — **The Glasgow Herald**

**Micah Clarke [1889]**

"This story strikes us as quite the best thing of its kind . . . since Lorna Doone." — **World**

"This is beyond all doubt the best historical story . . . since Mr. R. L. Stevenson's Kidnapped." — **Academy**

**The Sign of Four [1890]**

"Should be read by all who desire to improve their faculty of observation." — **Glamorgan Gazette**

**The White Company [1891]**

"We could not desire a more stirring romance . . . We feel throughout that Mr. Conan Doyle's story is not a mere item in the catalogue of exciting romances. It is real literature." — **Times**

"I have read nothing of the kind so good since 'Ivanhoe'." — **Illustrated London News**

"It is, in fact, as good a history of adventure and battles as we have read for a long time. Its interest rivals that of the best of Mr. R. L. Stevenson's stories, with this difference, that Mr. Doyle knows how to deal with the ladies of his dramatis personae." — **Observer**

"Mr. Conan Doyle writes an excellent style, pure and harmonious. There is absolutely no padding, and here and there passages of great beauty." — **Manchester Guardian**

**The Adventures of Sherlock Holmes [1892]**

"Of the dozen stories of which the book is made up there is not one which does not contain a thorough-paced mystery." — **Athenaeum**

"For those to whom the good, honest, breathless detective story is dear, Dr. Doyle's book will prove a veritable godsend." — **Athenaeum**

**Rodney Stone [1896]**

"The story goes so gallantly from start to finish that we are fairly startled out of our *fin de siecle* indifference and carried along in breathless excitement." — **Daily Telegraph**

"There is not a dull page in it from first to last. All is light, colour, movement, blended and inspired by a master hand." — **Punch**

"A notable and very brilliant work of genius." — **Speaker**

"Judged as a literary work I think it is his best, and as an exciting romance it would take a deal of beating . . . A beautifully written book!" — **Queen**

**Uncle Bernac [1897]**

"Uncle Bernac is for truth Dr. Doyle's Napoleon . . . it must take rank before anything he has written." — **Daily Chronicle**

"Uncle Bernac is a masterpiece . . ." — **World**

"It is not a small thing that we should have found amongst ourselves a writer who can thus interpret history for us." — **Speaker**

**The Tragedy of the Korosko [1898]**

"It is dangerous to describe any work of fiction in these days of a prolific press as a *masterpiece*, yet there cannot be any doubt that the word is strictly applicable to Mr. Conan Doyle's Tragedy of the Korosko." — **Speaker**

"A fine story, the interest of which arrests the reader's attention at the start and holds it to the close. The characterisation throughout is strong, clear and very delicate. Impressive, pulsating with emotion, informed with a great air of reality, this story will sustain and enhance its author's already high reputation." — **Daily News**

**Songs of Action [1898]**

"Doctor Doyle has well named his verse 'Songs of Action'. It pulsates with life and movement." — **Punch**

"Dr. Doyle has the gift of writing good rattling songs with all the swing of Rudyard Kipling." — **World**

"There is spirit and animation, the rush and glow of young blood about his poems." — **Daily Telegraph**

"Dr. Doyle's 'Songs' are songs of movement. They have fluency, they have vigour, they have force." — **Globe**

**The Great Boer War [1900]**

"It is difficult to read through 'The Great Boer War' by reason of the tears that dim the eyes as the sorrowful story is told. Conan Doyle made his reputation as a novelist; stranger far than fiction is the tale he has to tell of the campaign in South Africa . . His descriptions of the various engagements are masterpieces of graphic writing." — **Punch**

"Whatever histories of the war in South Africa are written, Dr. Conan Doyle's 'Great Boer War' must remain *the* history." — **Queen**

**The Green Flag and Other Stories of War and Sport [1900]**

"There is not a weak story or a dull page in this volume. Constructive skill, genuine humour, and a masterly style, combine to make this the most attractive volume of short stories . . ." — **Yorkshire Post**

"Few novelists of our time would have told the story in such stirring language . . . altogether the volume is admirable." — **Daily Telegraph**

**Songs of The Road [1911]**

"He is narrative, patriotic, dramatic — even philosophic." — **Times**

"The creator of Sherlock Holmes is able to construct vivid and pungent verse." — **Morning Post**

"Sir Arthur Conan Doyle has a very real gift as writer of verse. He can be vigorous in patriotic verse, boldly thoughtful in contemplative verse, and refreshingly humerous in narrative." — **Daily Telegraph**

"Typically Doylian, for the vigour, sense, and manliness he puts in all his work." — **Playgoer**

**Poems: Collected Edition [1922]**

"A verse-book full of keen zest . . ." — **Morning Post**

"Such ringing rhymes, and inspiring sentiments deserve to be popular." — **Daily Telegraph**

"His songs have a ring and a lilt of their own . . . there is vigour about his work which warms the blood." — **Sunday Times**

"He sings of noble deeds by land and sea . . . and inspiring lines urge us on to fresh endeavour." — **Daily Express**

**Acknowledgement**

I would like to thank Messrs. Harold Mortlake & Co. for their excellent catalogue No. 133 'Sherlock Holmes' (1969), which lists a large collection of books by Conan Doyle, including 627 Sherlockiana items. This collection was purchased by the Metropolitan Toronto Central Library. I have consulted this catalogue extensively, among numerous other sources, and found it most invaluable in preparing this not altogether simple bibliography. And it has certainly saved me a journey to Toronto!